S

TRICKS FOR
CATS

30 Fun and Easy Tricks You Can Teach Your Cat

Hollywood's Premier Animal Trainer

ANNE GORDON
with STEVE DUNO

PHOTOS BY DON MASON

ADAMS MEDIA CORPORATION
Holbrook, Massachusetts

Published by Adams Media Corporation,
260 Center Street, Holbrook, MA 02343

ISBN: 1-55850-613-6

Printed in the United States of America.

J   I   H   G   F   E   D   C   B   A

Library of Congress Cataloging-in-Publication Data
Gordon, Anne.
Show biz tricks for cats : 30 fun and easy tricks you can teach your cat /
by Hollywood's premier animal trainer Anne Gordon with Steve Duno.
p.   cm.
Includes index.
ISBN 1-55850-613-6 (pbk.)
1. Cats–Training. I. Duno, Steve. II. Title.
SF446.6.G67   1996
636.8'0888–dc20   96-10924
CIP

This publication is designed to provide accurate and authoritative information with regard to the subject matter covered. It is sold with the understanding that the publisher is not engaged in rendering legal, accounting, or other professional advice. If legal advice or other expert assistance is required, the services of a competent professional person should be sought.
— From a *Declaration of Principles* jointly adopted by a Committee of the American Bar Association and a Committee of Publishers and Associations

This book is available at quantity discounts for bulk purchases.
For information, call 1-800-872-5627 (in Massachusetts 617-767-8100).

Visit our home page at http://www.adamsmedia.com

ACKNOWLEDGMENTS

First and foremost, I would like to thank Steve Duno who phoned me one rainy January afternoon and suggested we write this book. A very special thank you goes to Don Mason for the generous donation of his photographic skills. A big thank you is extended to Debbie Betson, Heidi Sowards, and Judy Bishop who helped me train the cats for the photographs in this book. And most importantly, I want to thank Indy, Riley, Shadow, Raider, Oreo, Rudy, Sasha, Tigger, Levi, Willy, and Velvet who were patient with me and taught me how much fun it is to train cats.

To Mark and Dawn
who taught me the true meaning of
"colleague" and "friendship"

Contents

PREFACE

Many animal species have at some time been used by the entertainment industry. Animals have appeared in everything from commercials selling cars to feature films and television shows in which the animals are the stars. Trainers called upon to prepare these animals for their assignments have a difficult task before them. They must teach the animals to repeatedly perform difficult sequences of tasks under sometimes stressful conditions. The training techniques that evolve under such conditions have to be efficient, effective, and reliable. Television and film producers cannot afford to shoot a scene over and over again just to get a good shot of a cat sitting or jumping on cue. In the film and advertising industry, time is money. It must be done right the first time.

I have made my career training all types of animals to perform for the camera, including cats, dogs, wolves, deer, moose, raccoons, fox, bears, and tigers, and other large cats. My experiences over the years led me to develop the training techniques I use in this book; they meet the needs of an ever-demanding show business. The techniques are well thought out and detailed, and will produce the best results in the least amount of time. Over the years I have relied on them during countless shoots, and they have rarely let me down. If they work for me, they can work for you.

There are several reasons why you might want to consider training your cat to perform tricks. First, training is a great way to create a stronger bond between you and your cat. It will help build an attitude of mutual respect and trust between you. Second, it gives cats something to look forward to, helps relieve their boredom, and can reduce the stress of their being alone for long periods. Neither animals nor people should live a life of complacent routine, devoid of any learning experiences.

The tricks taught in this book use *positive* methods only; there is *no* negative reinforcement whatsoever.

There are always those who question the ethics of teaching a cat to sit, lie down, or come when called. They feel that it is an affront to the independent feline nature. First, understand that you will *never* get a cat to do something it does not *want* to do. Second, the fact is that all animals, including cats, learn many behaviors that are not instinctive but instead unique to their environments, mainly through conditioned response. Pavlov's dogs' salivating at the sound of a bell is the classic example. You train your cat all the time without even realizing it. A cat easily learns to come to the back door when its owner steps outside and taps on the top of a food can with a spoon. The same cat learns that the sound of an approaching car means *get out of the road!* Both are examples of conditioned response. Why not expand your cat's behavioral repertoire, thereby expanding its intellect?

With over thirty tricks to choose from, this book will help you do so. You should find teaching your cat some or all of these tricks to be a challenge, and a great way to build a closer bond between you. The learning experience will teach your cat to focus its thoughts, and will put you more closely in touch with the feline mind.

PART ONE

UNDERSTANDING YOUR CAT

Most cats in the wild live a solitary life. Unlike their canine cousins, wolves, dingoes, jackals, and coyotes, who live a much more social existence, the majority of wild cats come together only during the mating season or when territorial concerns lead to dominance contests. With the exception of lions, big cats do not rely on a team effort during hunting. The complex social interactions present in the pack hierarchy, so vital to the survival of canines, are for the most part nonexistent in the feline world.

The domestic house cat shares the same basic behavioral and social structure as its wild cousins. Your little tabby is much closer to being a leopard than you may realize. It stakes out its territory, surveys it from a high vantage point, and defends it against intrusions from others. It is a marvelous physical specimen. Its unique anatomical features allow it great agility, strength, and cunning. A perfect hunter, the domestic cat is able to quietly stalk and kill prey as efficiently as a wild cat. Your cat is also proportionately identical to many large cats, particularly the leopard and cougar. This cannot be said for the domestic canine; some breeds are so physically removed from wolves that the contrast is humorous.

Because their affiliation with other cats is primarily sexual or adversarial, not pack-oriented, cats learn differently from dogs. Your tabby has somewhat different priorities than Fido down the street. Pack loyalty among dogs is a strong drive; the individual actions of the members must coincide with the greater welfare of the pack. Canine behavior is normally directed toward the greater good and mediated by the pack leader, whose responsibility it is to maintain order, harmony, and equity among the group, as well as to orchestrate the hunt, control intrapack breeding practices, and meter out discipline when needed. Training a dog is relatively easy once you have established yourself as its pack leader, because the dog desires to please the leader, be it canine or human.

Pack loyalty is by no means a strong drive in cats; cats are far more narcissistic than dogs, and want to know "what's in it for me?". Domestic cats don't really belong to anyone the way dogs do. Receiving any form of discipline from an animal other than its mother is also a foreign concept to a cat; in the wild, there is no pack leader to tell cats what to do or how to behave. If your dog doesn't sit when you ask it to you can legitimately tell it "no" and perhaps give it a slight tug on the leash. This is known as negative reinforcement. Training methods like this just won't work on cats. To the contrary; punish a cat and it may never listen to you again.

This does not imply, however, that cats are antisocial. Quite the contrary is true. Cats bond to their owners in a parent/child fashion. They often see themselves as offspring that have not yet left you, the parent. This, rather than pack loyalty, is the source of your cat's bonding and affection.

Though cats do not vary in size nearly as widely as dogs, there can nevertheless be substantial weight variation, with cats ranging from a lithe four or five pounds right up to over twenty pounds for a spoiled fat cat. Cats have sharp, retractable claws that aid in climbing and defense, and canine-like teeth that allow them to tear and consume prey.

In addition to possessing phenomenal visual acuity, feline eyes also have the ability to gather light, allowing the cat to see well in near-pitch-black conditions. Though not completely color-blind, cats do not distinguish color as well as humans do. Their sense of hearing is excellent, but their sense of smell is adequate at best.

Cats are famous for their sense of balance. Most can walk across a one-inch-thick fence top without so much as a flinch. Try to get your beagle to do that! Cats also have an uncanny ability to right themselves in mid-fall, and will almost always land on all fours.

If pack loyalty is not a basic drive in cats, then what is? There are three areas that cats find instinctively motivating:

1. *Sex.* The desire to mate has an elemental effect on a cat's behavior. Animals that are not altered will be motivated to go out and find another cat to mate with. Males will often fight other males to secure access to a female. The domestic cat is able to produce young at a prodigious rate; the female can come into heat as often

as every two weeks, and can begin mating again as soon as one month after the weaning of a litter. The male cat is able to breed year-round.

As you can see, if you choose to own a cat (especially if it will be outside part of the time), you will do yourself a great service by having it altered. Neutering (castration of the male), and spaying (removal of the female's ovaries and uterus) are simple procedures that will prevent the unwanted and often tragic production of kittens. Males will tend to fight, roam, and mark less, and females will have a lesser chance of developing uterine and breast cancer.

The sex drive is not a drive that can be harnessed for our purposes of training. It can in fact prevent you from getting much done at all. Do yourself and your cat a favor and have it altered.

2.   *Territoriality.* Both wild and domestic cats are very territorial. The cat's territory is really its hunting ground, and it is prized because within it is the prey the cat needs to survive. Though canines also tend to be quite territorial, their territories tend to expand, contract, or move according to season, competition, and availability of prey. Solitary felines tend to establish more permanent hunting areas and to guard them more zealously than do canines. This territorial drive is directed primarily toward other cats. You may have observed this territoriality between your cat and a neighbor's, or perhaps when bringing a new kitten or puppy into your own home. The resident cat can be downright cruel to the new arrival for months, until some territorial compromise is worked out.

The size of a domestic cat's assumed territory depends largely on its level of dominance; if it thinks it deserves a huge "kingdom" then it will covet the largest area possible, usually getting into a fight or two along the way. Like the sexual drive, the territorial drive will not be extremely useful to you in terms of training.

3. *Food.* The desire to hunt and eat is another strong primary drive in cats. It is also the cornerstone to training any feline, be it a tiger or a tabby. Cats are charming narcissists; offering an irresistible treat can work wonders in motivating them to perform, especially if it is close to feeding time. This is the one drive that we will take full advantage of in the training process. Some cats have a higher food drive than others; these are great cats to teach tricks to because they will do anything for food. Let's hope you have a cat with a high food drive, for it will accelerate the learning process greatly. Experiment with different treats to see if there is a special kind that your cat really loves.

Though your cat's diet hopefully consists of a good-quality pet food and not unfortunate creatures found outside, the basic idea is the same; food is of great concern to your feline. Cats are carnivores to an even greater extent than are dogs, who in the wild do often consume some plant material. Cats need a higher percentage of protein in their diet than do dogs. Any good quality cat food, be it dry or canned, should provide your cat with essential protein, as well as vitamins, minerals, fatty acids, and carbohydrates.

Intelligence, though hard to define and quantify, plays a key role in how efficiently any animal learns new behaviors. How smart you think a person is depends on what criteria you are using at any given time. For example, if you were to give a test on farming techniques to a group of city-dwellers, chances are they would score poorly. This does not mean they are unintelligent.

The same goes for animals. Many people like to compare dogs and cats and conclude that dogs are smarter because of all they are capable of doing. After all, dogs can hunt, herd, retrieve, work as rescue or protection animals, aid people with a variety of disabilities . . . the list is endless. What can cats do?

This is not a fair comparison. First, dogs have a long history of working closely with humans. Cats do not. Humans and dogs are both social animals and therefore have a more basic understanding of each other's behavior patterns. Dogs also have had thousands of years to develop complex behaviors that we choose to identify as "intelligent." They have been genetically manipulated far more than cats to better suit particular roles. Just look at the size differential between a Chihuahua and a Great Dane! Such dramatic physical differences do not exist in the domestic cat because, historically, there was never a need to genetically "craft" cats to perform a myriad of specific duties.

Cats have worked with humans only as ratters, a behavior that comes instinctively to them, requiring no instruction from us. The fact that dogs have been taught to do so many things gives them the appearance of being better problem solvers than cats. This has contributed to the belief that dogs are smart and that cats cannot be trained.

In actuality, dogs *must* be trained in order to live amicably with humans. Cats do not need much training at all. They usually teach themselves to use a litter box, and instinctively clean themselves. They are for the most part self-regulating, not needing constant input from their owners the way dogs do.

Animals learn in much the same way we do; they observe, interpret what they have seen, then act upon it. When an action turns out to be the wrong one, the animal learns from the error. Trial and error therefore occurs with all animal species, including cats. While teaching tricks to your cat, you will learn to use the method known as "conditioned response." Simply put, when your cat performs the desired action, it gets rewarded, whereas its improper responses simply get ignored. Your cat will quickly learn to perform the trick because of the pleasing consequences.

The ease of cat ownership has contributed to the belief that cats cannot be trained, that they in fact need to be left to their own devices. On the contrary, *cats are intelligent*, and *can be trained*, but not in the same fashion as dogs. You will never get cats to do something they do not want to do. The challenge is to make them think that *performing the trick is to their advantage*.

🐾 🐾 🐾

Cats, just like dogs, communicate vocally, bodily, and through scent markers. When two cats are approaching each other, they will sometimes vocalize their intentions to each other. Friendly meetings are generally silent, with tails and ears up. Each cat normally sniffs the other thoroughly. Real confrontation may be heralded by guttural sounds or even threatening hisses. Cats will also vocalize during mating; females will often emit a horrifying wail at the end of copulation, sounding very much like a baby screaming.

Body posturing is also an important tool in cat communication. We have all at one point seen a frightened cat go into a severely arched posture, baring its fangs and hissing away. This is easily interpreted as saying "I'm really scared; go away or I'll hurt you." Other signs of feline apprehension include a thrashing tail, dropped-back ears, hair standing on end (a cat's attempt to make itself look larger), or prolonged eye contact. Conversely, when your cat lies purring in your lap and kneads at you with its front paws, you instinctively know that it is happy and content (this kneading action is a behavior first begun by the kitten while nursing; the kneading action stimulates the flow of milk). Additional signs of contentment include purring, rubbing, a vertically raised tail, and stretching.

Cats also communicate to other cats through scent marking. The easiest way to mark territorial boundaries is through urine spraying or defecation. This strong statement to others draws an imaginary "line in the sand" for other cats to smell and heed.

Teaching tricks to your cat should be fun for both of you. Cats will not respond to training methods that involve punishment of any kind. *Never yell at or hit a cat.* Lose your cool and you may lose your cat's trust forever.

A cat will do nothing it does not want to do. Believe me. You must convince your cat that performing tricks is a pathway to great pleasure, in this case, wonderful food. Food is the key to teaching a cat to do anything. Only if you reward your cat with its favorite treats will you see results. The degree of success you ultimately have with your cat depends more on the patience you have than on your training expertise.

You must have patience while teaching tricks to your cat. Remember, though cats do learn through trial and error, they nevertheless are not programmed to learn in quite the same fashion as dogs or humans. They will not perform out of a sense of pack loyalty, but only out of a desire for food. Their ability and desire to focus on a specific task will be far less than that of a dog or a human, as well. Take this instinctive trait into consideration when training. Never adopt a serious, militant attitude. It is all for fun.

Some cats will learn more quickly than others. Those with high food drives and those that are courageous and curious will fare better than timid or aloof cats. You can, however, still work with what you have; any cat can learn. The tricks in this book are numerous; some of them may be more appealing to your cat than others, so experiment and see which work best.

PART TWO
GETTING STARTED

YOUR CAT: THE STAR OF THE SHOW

The first and most important element in the training process is your cat. Almost any cat can be trained to perform tricks quite well. Several factors, however, will affect how well your cat learns.

Breed

There are numerous cat breeds to choose from, ranging from the short-haired, puma-like Abyssinian to the beautiful long-haired Persian. They all make great pets and can all learn. Unlike the more genetically manipulated dog, most breeds of cat have about the same level of intelligence. There are a few, however, that do seem slightly more willing to work. Siamese cats are extra-friendly, having an almost dog-like desire for affection and interaction. They also love to climb, which can help with some tricks. The popular tabby is also very willing and affectionate. Calicoes and tortoise-shells, however, can sometimes act aloof and uncooperative. Abyssinians, though affectionate with their owners, can be a bit shy around strangers, sometimes exhibiting an almost feral temperament. Overall, though, trainability among the different cat breeds is fairly consistent, certainly much more so than in dogs.

Long-haired cats such as the Persian, Himalayan, and Angora may have more problems with hairballs than the short-haired breeds, but may also tend to be a bit mellower than their short-haired cousins. Short-haired cats may be better at certain agility tricks and at the "Come" command, because of a slightly higher energy level.

Size differs somewhat in cats, but again, not nearly as much as in dogs. The Maine coon, for instance, is a thick-boned cat that can often weigh over twenty pounds, whereas the Hairless Sphinx tends to be much lighter and thinner.

Age

The age of your cat will have some effect on its ability to learn. Generally, the older a cat is, the longer it will take to learn new behaviors. Adult cats over the age of four or five are more set in their ways and have had years in which to "perfect" their own catalog of behaviors. With patience, however, you should not have much trouble getting an older cat to learn. The key is that these tricks are *new* behaviors, not replacement behaviors for bad habits picked up over the years. Changing a behavior in any animal is harder than teaching a new one.

Kittens and young adult cats up to the age of one year will generally be the best students. They have fewer established behaviors and are much more impressionable. They have not yet taught themselves a way of learning in the manner that older cats have.

A kitten, however, will be much more active than an adult; it will therefore get into more trouble and take up more of your time. Kittens also eat and eliminate more often. Adults sleep more, and are generally more easygoing. Regardless of the age of the cat you have, though, you can teach your cat that it is fun to learn.

History

The background or history of your cat is also a factor in the learning process. First, was it well-socialized with humans and cats during its kitten-hood? A kitten that has had early and frequent exposure to people, cats, and even dogs is more likely to become a willing, confident student than a cat that has experienced an isolated beginning. The age that a kitten is adopted at plays a big role in its future behavior. Many kittens are adopted at far too young an age, and do not get a chance to learn how to properly socialize with other cats. If a kitten that has left the litter before it is seven to eight weeks old does not receive any further social-ization, it may show exaggerated hostility toward other ani-mals, particularly cats. At the least, it will be timid and insecure. When I was training animals for school, I once raised a tiger cub that had been pulled from its mother at three weeks of age; I had to bottle-feed it for several weeks and really play mother to it. This kitten nevertheless devel-oped an insecure habit, and would spend hours curled up in a corner, sucking on the end of its tail.

The size of the litter that a cat comes from can affect its level of comfort with other cats; those from a very small litter or those removed from their litter too early may not be as sociable with other cats. Sociability with humans is of even higher importance; a cat that panics whenever someone comes near it probably doesn't have enough confidence to master tricks with ease.

Where did you get your cat? Street cats may be a bit more wary and less socialized than cats purchased from a breeder. They have had a harder life, and may need time to acclimate to their new surroundings before training begins. You never know how much neglect or abuse a cat has experienced before you take it home. A cat that has been isolated or abused is harder to train than a well-adjusted cat.

Most of my cats come from shelters. I'm a real sucker for the "down and out" type. Sasha, one of my best performers, came from a shelter, and, after a few months of getting used to me and my home, began work on the set of *Home for the Holidays*.

Teaching a shy or timid cat to perform tricks can actually be therapeutic, effectively raising its confidence level. During the training, the cat will get regular praise and reinforcement, just the right type of medicine for an unsure feline.

Gender

Most big cats that I have trained for films, television shows, and commercials have been males. These large animals are never altered, primarily due to their status as endangered species. They must be bred to help preserve the species. In my experience, unaltered female lions and tigers tend to worry more than their male counterparts, particularly during estrus, or if they have cubs. Though playing only a minor role in the training process for domestic cats, the gender of your pet will have a small effect on the procedure. Male cats tend to be a bit more confident and curious and may learn faster than females. Females can be a bit more aloof at first, especially when other pets are present, and may be somewhat less daring. Overall, though, gender-related behavioral differences in the domestic cat will be negligible.

Health

The general health of your cat must be of primary consideration. An animal suffering from medical problems such as kidney disease, urinary tract infection, feline leukemia, or arthritis will not be motivated to learn, for obvious reasons. Make sure your cat is healthy and pain-free before you begin any training.

In order to determine if your cat is healthy, you must have on hand the services of a good veterinarian. A new cat or kitten should be taken to the vet soon after its homecoming. If you don't already have a good vet in mind, attempt to choose one before the cat comes home. Consult friends with healthy cats when deciding on a good vet, rather than choosing one at random. Your vet will assess your new cat's general health and also properly vaccinate it against potentially lethal diseases such as distemper, rhinotracheitis, feline leukemia, calicivirus and rabies. Extreme lethargy, loss of appetite, diarrhea, or rapid respiration can be signs of a very sick cat; if any of these symptoms arise, see your vet immediately.

Good nutrition is vital to the health of your cat. Feed it a good quality dry food, and supplement with canned food if you desire (though this is generally not necessary; dry foods contain all needed nutrients and are cheaper than canned foods, which tend to contain high amounts of water). Cats with kidney or urinary tract problems, however, may need to avoid dry food which could tend to exacerbate the condition. If in doubt, speak to your vet. Follow the manufacturer's directions regarding amounts, but take into consideration whether or not your cat is altered; if it is, you may need to reduce the amount of food given by about 10 percent to prevent obesity. Also realize that you will be using an appreciable amount of treats during the training process laid out in Part Three of this book. You will need to reduce your cat's meals accordingly, to avoid ending up with a fat cat.

Some cats can develop food allergies. Just as humans can be allergic to foods such as milk, beef, pork, corn, or rice, so too can cats. Signs of food allergy in a cat might include vomiting, skin problems, or diarrhea. If you see these or any other unusual symptoms, consult your vet, who may prescribe a special diet to alleviate the condition.

Always provide your cat with fresh water, even at night. Most cats are somewhat active at night, and will need refreshment.

Later in the book, we will discuss feeding schedules, and how they will tie in with the training process.

EQUIPMENT YOU WILL NEED

You will need to purchase several pieces of equipment before you begin training your cat. I will cover them one at a time:

Collar

Though not essential to the training process, I recommend you keep a collar on your cat, primarily as a place to attach some form of identification. Most people will gladly call the owner of a found cat if they find a phone number on a tag hanging from the cat's collar. Good pet shops sell cat collars. Consider purchasing an elastic collar that stretches if caught on something, preventing the cat from panicking or choking.

Clicker

The clicker, a metal
or plastic sound-
making device
available in toy or
novelty stores, is
an important train-
ing device. The
"click" acts as a
bridge between the
desired behavior and
the reward. Trainers
who work with dol-
phins use a whistle
much in the same

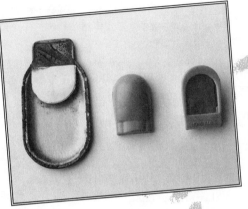

way that I use the clicker, blowing it as soon as the dolphin
performs a trick correctly. For example, when the dolphin is
at the apex of a jump, the trainer will blow the whistle,
telling the dolphin that it performed perfectly. This is always
followed by a food reward. I use the clicker because it pro-
duces a very identifiable, unique sound that is short in
duration and not too loud. Using the clicker for the behavior bridge also frees up the use of a whistle for other training needs, such as teaching the "Come" command. You will
use the clicker *immediately* before rewarding your cat for
properly performing a trick. The clicking sound is soon
interpreted by your cat as meaning "Yes, that's right, good
job!" It will also heighten the cat's expectations for the food
treat that follows. The click eventually becomes as important as the food treat because it creates a mood of excited
expectation.

Sound-Making Device

A referee's whistle, commonly found in most toy or sporting goods stores, will do nicely to help teach the "Come" command. Other sound-making devices, such as a bicycle bell or an electric buzzer, will also work well. Whatever sound you decide to use, it

should be easily heard but not overwhelming to the cat. A whistle works well because you can vary the volume by the force of your breath. If your cat spends time outside, more volume may be necessary. Inside, a lower volume is preferred.

Various Toys

Any toys that your cat really loves can be used as motivational tools, and will be very useful when teaching your

cat the "Fetch" command. A crocheted ball is a favorite with many cats, as is a fake mouse. Teaser toys, such as a fabric mouse on a string or feathers attached to a wand, can be use-

ful when teaching your cat to
"Rise," "Jump," or "Spin."

Travel Crate

One of the handiest items I
own is a small plastic traveling
crate for my cats. It is an essential
piece of equipment if you intend
to travel with your cat, be it on a
plane or in the car. There is nothing more unsettling and
dangerous for a driver than a panicked cat loose in a moving
vehicle. A crate will keep the cat calm and secure during
unpredictable, hectic situations. I feel that plastic travel
crates, recommended by airline carriers, are the best choice
for transporting your cat. This type of crate provides your
cat with a high degree of security and safety; it is sturdy yet
does not make the cat feel as if it were in a "fish bowl" the
way wire cages can. A wire cage restrains the cat but makes
it feel vulnerable, whereas a plastic crate, by being closed in
on three sides, creates a more snug feeling for your pet.

Teaching your cat to accept going into a plastic travel
crate can be an extremely useful tool. I recommend that you

teach your cat to go into and
feel comfortable in a plastic
travel crate if you ever intend
to travel by car or plane with
your cat. A trip to the vet or
an extended car journey can
be made much simpler if you
do this. This behavior should
start when the cat is young.

Here is how to acclimate your cat to its traveling crate.

1. Place the cat in the crate. Close the door and leave it closed for a few minutes. Then open it and give the cat a very special treat, perhaps a piece of cheese or tuna.

2. Gradually lengthen the amount of time the cat spends in the crate.

3. Once the cat is comfortably going into the crate, try taking it (in the crate) for a short car ride around the block. Over a period of a few weeks, you can gradually increase the distance covered until a trip to the vet or Grandma's is no big deal. Don't take your cat in the car, though, if it is an extremely hot day. The cat could easily overheat and panic. After the ride is over, carry the crate into the home, release the cat, then reward it.

Treats

A wide variety of treats can be used to entice your cat into performing tricks. I have found that a spoonful of meat-flavored baby food works best with my cats. The spoon is a handy tool that can be offered and removed quickly. It also allows you to use certain gooey treats that might be hard to hold in your hand. I start with a spoonful of the food, allowing the cat to eat a portion of it each time it responds correctly.

Bits of cheese, chicken, or tuna also work well. Use whatever your cat is crazy for. Each treat should be small enough for your cat to eat very quickly. A large treat will cause your cat to go off in a corner to eat it at its leisure, so try to avoid this. Do not use your cat's regular food; it gets this too regularly for it to be special enough.

Other Props

Some of the tricks in this book require the use of certain props. The following will be needed if you decide to teach the corresponding tricks:

Hoop and pedestals

Available at most pet shops or easily constructed with a hula hoop and two footstools, these with be needed for the "Through a Hoop" trick.

Stepladders

One stepladder will be needed for the "Climb Ladder" trick, and two will be needed for the "Balance Beam" trick. Both should be three or four steps high.

Balance Beam

A wooden board about four feet long and four inches wide will be needed to teach the "Balance Beam" trick. A board of equal length and two inches in width can also be used as the cat progresses.

Bell

A small bell on a string or a larger ship's bell mounted on a wooden stand, will be needed to teach the "Ring It" trick. Small bells can be found in most toy or novelty stores, and larger bells can be purchased in marine supply stores.

CREATING THE APPROPRIATE ENVIRONMENT

Always begin teaching tricks in a quiet room with *no* distractions whatsoever. No other persons or animals should be present. Televisions, radios, washers, and dryers should all be turned off. Choose the room that is farthest from street traffic, and pick a quiet part of the day. Cats are highly curious animals and will lose focus on the lesson if anything else is going on. Only after the trick has been mastered by your cat should you begin to slowly introduce distractions.

I usually work my cats on a table or desk rather than on the floor because cats prefer being up high. Standing during the session is also easier on your back. Training sessions are normally most productive right before dinnertime, when the cat is most likely to be food-motivated.

A word on feeding practices as they relate to the training: Most cat owners free-feed their cats, leaving food down all the time and allowing their pets to eat when they choose. There is nothing wrong with this method. However, I have found that the use of specific feeding times helps me better predict when my cats will be hungry. I then schedule a training session right before feeding time to ensure that my cats will be most motivated to perform for treats. By feeding your cat at specific times, you actually program it to be hungry at a specific time. The cat will learn to associate correctly performing a trick with satiating itself. If you find that your cat is not very treat-motivated, then try changing from free-feeding to specific feeding times. Leave the cat's food down for thirty minutes, then remove whatever is left, saving it for the next feeding. Your cat will quickly realize that there is now a smaller window of time in which to eat. This method invigorates your cat's appetite and increases its motivation and focus during training sessions.

ACCLIMATING TO TOUCH

During the training sessions, your cat will need to tolerate a lot of handling. Some cats won't like this; I recommend that, from early on, you begin desensitizing your cat to touch. Teaching your cat from a very early age to accept full body massage is the best way to do this. It will eventually have a calming effect on the cat, and will put you in touch with your pet's body. Often, a cat will have a problem such as arthritis, a pulled muscle, or a fatty tumor that will go unnoticed by the owner due to the cat's innate ability to mask pain. Massage will reveal these problems to you, largely by your cat's showing marked discomfort when having the problem area rubbed.

Offer your cat a large treat in your right hand; while the cat is eating it, massage its neck gently with your left hand while talking quietly. Slowly work down the body using light, circular motions. Also, don't forget to lightly handle the feet. Try to include massage fairly often; once per day for just a minute or two will succeed in desensitizing your cat to handling. Within a few weeks, your cat should readily accept it, unless it *absolutely hates* being handled. If you do have an "untouchable" cat, then don't push the massage issue.

Also try carrying your cat around the house while intermittently feeding it bits of cheese or tuna. Handle its feet and tail, and always follow it up with a treat. Eventually your cat will grow to tolerate and even enjoy these handling sessions.

WALKING ON A LEASH

Many owners allow their cats to be outside on their own during a good part of the day. In a busy urban or suburban environment, this can be deadly. At the very least, a cat that spends time outside can acquire parasites, get into fights with other cats, get hit by cars, mauled by dogs, or reproduce haphazardly. So can an owner safely get his or her cat outside to enjoy the day? Perhaps. Some say the answer is to teach the cat to walk on a leash, so that the experience can be controlled by you, the owner. I tend to disagree, and I'll explain why.

Try to understand the feline nature. Cats are in ways much more elemental than dogs—they are closer to being wild animals than a beagle or basset ever will be. They determine that situations are dangerous much more quickly than dogs, and will invariably want to retreat from these perceived dangers. Also, cats will define many more situations as dangerous than will dogs. When you combine this almost feral level of perception with having a cat out in public on a leash, you could have the ingredients for trouble. Many cat owners live in large cities; I believe this to be a poor environment to walk a cat in. Requiring a cat to walk, under restraint, down a street with buses and backfires and hundreds of pedestrians rushing by is too much to ask, in my opinion. A panicked cat on the end of a leash is not an easy experience to deal with, believe me. The cat could end up hurting itself or you, badly. At the very least, it will lose trust in you. If you live in a quiet rural area, you could probably be fairly successful, but I cannot recommend that you attempt walking a cat on a leash for long periods of time. Unlike dogs, cats can be totally content to stay inside (a safer option), and this is what I would recommend.

USING A FLUSH TOILET

Some cat owners that I know have professed a desire to teach their cats to use a flush toilet instead of a litter box. The advantages are the elimination of the litter box and its sometimes offensive mess and odor, as well as the expense of litter. The disadvantages to having your cat use the toilet bowl are the embarrassment of having guests stumble upon the act or its aftermath, always having to keep the lid up, and the possibility of your cat's missing the mark.

Personally, I use several litter boxes for my cats, and keep them as clean as possible. I have found that odor can be kept down to a minimum if you simply scoop often and change the litter regularly.

If you decide that you would like to teach your cat to use the toilet bowl, you will need several pieces of equipment to make the training possible. Rather than explain to you how to make these from scratch, I recommend that to save some time and effort, you visit your local pet shop and purchase a ready-made kit. Several manufacturers distribute these kits in quality pet shops nationwide; they actually work quite well if you follow the instructions exactly.

Most of these kits include a plastic litter container that clips onto the toilet seat, so that it perches squarely in the middle of the opening. You start by filling it with litter and gradually decreasing the amount of litter. Eventually you remove the plastic litter container entirely, so that the cat begins eliminating directly into the bowl. The challenge is to go through the procedure gradually, over a period of weeks.

If this interests you, purchase one of these kits and give it a try. It will be much easier than rigging up your own system. If you have a second bathroom, train the cat to perform this "trick" in there, instead of in your bathroom.

PART THREE
THE TRICKS

I start off with the most basic tricks and work up to some that are slightly more difficult to teach. Each cat learns differently, however, and may find a "hard" trick easy or an "easy" one difficult. The cat's personality, likes, and dislikes will determine what it excels at.

The instructions given here are fairly simple. Each trick features an indicator that tells the level of difficulty (from one to four paws), what you will need to teach it, length and frequency of sessions, advance preparation (if any), and previous tricks required. The photos provided will help you get a feeling for the proper positioning of the cat and yourself, as well as the correct placement of the treat. You will quickly discover that because your cat is an individual, certain instructions may have to be tailored to fit your situation. For example, some cats need to have the treat closer to their noses than others. Others may require you to move the treat faster, or perhaps more slowly. You will learn this once you begin learning how your cat learns.

BASIC RULES OF TRAINING YOUR CAT

1. Never physically hit your cat or get angry at it. If necessary, use a spray bottle filled with water to dissuade the cat from continuing whatever trouble it has gotten into.

2. Always start a trick in a quiet area free of distractions.

3. Remember to teach your cat when it is hungry.

4. Work only one trick at a time during the learning phase. If your cat hasn't mastered "Sit," for example, do not move on to "Stand" or any other trick.

5. Precede each command with your cat's name.

6. *Always* reward a cat with a treat when it performs a trick.

7. Remember to use the release word "Okay" to release your cat from all sessions.

8. Always end your training sessions on a positive note!

9. Don't force your cat to do anything it doesn't care to do. If it isn't comfortable being held, for example, then you shouldn't work the "Snuggle" command.

10. Do not overwork your cat: follow the "Length of Session" and "Frequency of Sessions" guidelines.

11. Once your cat learns a trick, continue working it at least once every week, to keep it fresh in the cat's mind.

12. Change the type of treats you are using every so often, so that your cat doesn't get bored.

13. Teach your cat in different places; otherwise it will quickly learn to anticipate the reward because of *where it is* and not *what it is doing.*

14. One person should perfect a trick with the cat before another person attempts to work that same trick.

15. Don't forget to have fun with your cat!

Trick No. 1
Sit

I recently finished working on the set of the feature film *Home for the Holidays*, directed by Jodie Foster. Jodie required that a cat be in several scenes; it had to "Sit" and "Stay" for periods of time while scenes were shot. I brought in Sasha, my long-haired tabby, to play the role of "Fat Frank."

One of the scenes was shot in a large room with many cast and crew members present.

During the first rehearsal it was obvious to me that most of the people present were skeptical of my chances of getting Sasha to perform on cue. Many of them had talked to me previously about cats they had owned; they could not imagine their cats doing anything on command.

Level of difficulty:

What you will need:
a clicker and treats

Length of session:
five to ten minutes

Frequency of sessions:
two to three times every day

Advance preparation:
none

Previous tricks required:

Just before the scene began, I brought Sasha over to her spot and gave her the "Sit" command, which she promptly obeyed and was rewarded for. The room filled with murmurs of "Oh wow" and "Fantastic!" Jodie was just as surprised and asked me several times, "Does she really *listen* to you?" Later, after seeing the cat perform in numerous scenes, she commented to the cast and crew that "This cat works better than most actors." Some of the actors weren't exactly jumping for joy over that comment, but they all took it in stride.

The "Sit" command is the building block for all other commands you will teach your cat. When you begin teaching it to your cat, you will actually be teaching it *how to learn* instead of just react to stimuli. The most important moment in the training of your cat will be the first time your cat sits when you ask it to. In order for you to move on to any other commands, your cat must first master "Sit."

1. Choose a quiet room, preferably in the back of the home, away from street noises. Place the cat on a table, away from the edge. First get the cat to stand, if it isn't already, by petting it on its rump. Most cats will instinctively raise their rumps when you do this.

2. Hold a treat an inch or two in front of the

cat's nose. Do not let it eat any yet; just let it get a good whiff. The cat's focus should be on the food and the anticipation of eating it.

3. As soon as the cat shows interest and focus, slowly move the food along an invisible line drawn from the cat's nose to a point right between its ears. As you do this, say your cat's name and then say "Sit." Make sure the food is never more than an inch or two from the cat's head or it may stand up, come forward for the food, or rise up on its back legs for it. If

the cat is hungry enough, you should be able to get it to sit within five to ten attempts. If not, stop and try again in fifteen minutes. Also, reevaluate the treat you are using. Perhaps it is not appealing to your cat. During this you will be learning the fine art of treat manipulation; where you place the treat and how you move it will have a direct effect on the performance of the cat. *Make sure you attempt the training when the cat is hungry.* If you haven't as yet changed to specific feeding times, now is the time to start. Remember, if you can predict when your cat will be hungry then you can motivate it to work for treats. You will see a difference in the cat's response to the training.

4. The *moment* your cat does sit, click your clicker once, say "Good Sit," and *immediately* give your cat the treat. If you are using a spoonful of food, let the cat have just a bite each time it successfully performs the trick. When

your cat has successfully sat three or four times, end the session by saying "Okay!" This lets it know that the work is over and it can relax for a bit. I also always pet the cat in conjunction with saying "Okay."

5. Give your cat lots of love and then feed it its meal. Do not have another session until right before the next feed-

ing time. Work the "Sit" at least twice each day; after a week or so, the cat should begin understanding what it is you are asking of it. Once your cat is sitting regularly on command, try giving the command once without the treat present to see if your pet truly understands. If the cat sits, click the clicker, wait a few moments, then give it a reward and lots of love. Remember that the food reward should continue as a regular part of the training. Unlike with dogs, you will not be able to completely eliminate treats from the process, even after the cat has mastered the trick. Above all, *be patient.*

TRICK NO. 2
STAND

"Stand" is a relatively easy command to teach most cats. I use it sometimes on shoots, usually as a precursor to the cat's coming to me across a room or field. Many film shots require a cat to be standing and observing some activity. Also, print photography may require a cat to appear to be doing something such as riding a surfboard. Situations like this require me to actually train a cat to perform a "Stand/Stay" on a surfboard or some other prop long enough for the photographer to shoot a few rolls of film.

You will have quick results with this one, as long as your cat likes to be touched.

Level of difficulty:
🐾

What you will need:
a clicker and treats

Length of session:
five minutes

Frequency of sessions:
four to five times every day

Advance preparation:
none

Previous tricks required:

1. Start with your cat in the "Sit" position on a table, away from the edge. Make sure the room is quiet, with no distractions.

2. Say the cat's name followed by the command "Stand," then immediately pet or scratch the cat on its rump, right above the base of the tail. All cats will instinctively raise up their rumps in response to this.

3. As soon as the cat rises into the "Stand" position, click your clicker, reward the cat with a treat, and say "Good Stand." Work this three or four times and then quit for the day.

4. Eventually you will be able to stop scratching the cat's rump to get it to stand; it will begin associating the spoken command word with the desired action, as long as the treat always follows. Be patient, and practice every day.

5. Once the cat is regularly performing the "Stand," you can begin adding the "Stay" command to it, gradually backing yourself away from the cat while repeating "Good Stay" and using the hand signal. Keep in mind, though, that when a cat is in a "Stand," it will be poised for action, so "Stay" will initially be an alien concept for it. If the cat breaks the position, just go back to it, repeat the "Stand" command, say "Stay," and back away again, perhaps a bit more slowly this time.

6. End the session after several successful attempts. Release the cat with an "Okay," then pick it up and give it a kiss.

**Teach the cat in different places;
otherwise it may only perform a trick
in only one spot.**

TRICK NO. 3
SNUGGLE

For some cats, snuggling with their owner is no trick at all. Many cats love being held in your arms. My cat Rudy is one of these cats. He loves being held, and will actually be a pest about it. If I am standing near a counter that he is on, he will leap into my arms whether I am prepared for him or not. I once had a local news reporter here in my house to do an interview; Rudy would not leave her alone. He pestered her mercilessly until she conceded her lap to him. Once there, he purred away happily.

Other cats, however, dislike being held. Unlike Rudy, my cat Raider hates being held, even for a few seconds. She was

Level of difficulty:

What you will need:
a clicker, treats, and a helper

Length of session:
five to ten minutes

Frequency of sessions:
three to four times every day

Advance preparation:
none

Previous tricks required:

roughly handled by some small children during her kitten-hood, and has never cared for snuggling since. Sasha, the cat used in *Home for the Holidays*, tolerates being held for short periods only, and gets very tired of it after about two minutes. Holly Hunter did a terrific job when it came to handling Sasha, who would get fidgety whenever I was close by. Holly would patiently walk away with Sasha and calm her down so that we could shoot the scene.

Begin handling your cat from the time it is a kitten. An adopted adult cat that does not like to be handled will proba-bly not ever like it. If your cat tends to be this way, then you might consider skipping the "Snuggle" trick. If you have a cat like Sasha, however, you can condition it to tolerate and even appreciate being held for longer and longer periods of time.

1. Have a helper pick up and snuggle your cat. You should be right next to them, holding your clicker in one hand and a treat in the other. Do not let your cat see the treat yet.

2. If your cat starts to fidget, have your helper gently squeeze it (not too hard) until it stops fidgeting. Your helper should release the pres-sure as soon as the

cat relaxes, while you click your clicker once and then reward the cat. You can verbally praise the cat by saying "Good Snuggle." At this point the cat should be more focused on the treat to come than on getting out of the helper's arms.

3. Slowly extend the time your cat is held. Have your helper carry the cat around the room and return to you before you click and reward.

4. You, of course, should also practice holding the cat yourself. The reason for using the helper is twofold; first, it frees your hands, enabling you to click and reward. It also desensitizes the cat to being handled by strangers.

5. Recruit friends to practice holding the cat while you reward it.

Remember never to click and reward if the cat is squirming or fighting. Only reward when the cat is relaxed and settled.

TRICK NO. 4

SPIN

This should be a fairly easy trick to teach your cat. The behavior is simple; the cat will spin around in a tight circle, almost as if it were chasing its own tail.

Level of difficulty:
✦✦

What you will need:
a clicker and treats

Length of session:
two to three minutes

Frequency of sessions:
two to three times every day

Advance preparation:
none

Previous tricks required:
none

1. Start with the cat standing on the floor in front of you. You can be on your knees or standing.

2. Let the cat see that you have a very special treat in hand. Hold it close to the cat's nose, then guide the cat around in a tight circle as you say "Spin." Don't pull the treat more than a few inches away from the cat's nose at any time. If the cat does follow the treat around, click once and reward. Don't worry about speed at this point; just work on getting the cat to follow the treat. Continue working on this step until the cat spins around every time. Also, attempt to increase the speed at which the cat spins.

3. Begin to slowly increase your distance from the cat, a few inches at a time. You have been using a large circular motion with your treat hand; this motion becomes the hand signal for "Spin." As you

get farther away from the cat, use this circular hand motion, but decrease the size of the circle you make. The objective here is to get the cat to spin around without having to actually be led by the treat. You should be able to ultimately give the verbal and hand cues for "Spin" from several feet away, and have the cat spin around on its own. Remember to take it slowly, and realize that the cat has to make the discovery that, if it per-

forms a specific behavior, it will be rewarded. After the cat masters the "Spin" trick going in one direction, try teaching it to "Spin" the other way.

**Remember: never overwork your cat;
follow the "Length of Session" recommendations,
and always end on a positive note!**

TRICK NO. 5
SHAKE

Most wild animals and many cats do not appreciate having their feet handled or held. Wild animals' feet are their first means of escape from danger; if their feet are injured or restrained in any way, they will not be able to flee. A cat may panic if the "Shake" command is taught improperly.

Level of difficulty:

What you will need:
a clicker and treats

Length of session:
one to five minutes

Frequency of sessions:
three to four times every day

Advance preparation:
none

Previous trick required:
Sit

Dogs are different; they have a higher desire to please their owners, and are farther removed from their "wild" side. Cats are more elemental, which is one of the reasons we love them so much. You must take care to never create a situation in which the cat feels trapped or threatened.

As with "Snuggle," some cats just will not tolerate this type of handling. Others, however, will let you touch them and hold them to your heart's content. I call these cats "clay kitties"; you can mold them into any position and they just love it. If you have a cat like this, then "Shake" will be easy to teach.

1. Start with your cat in a sitting position, close to the edge of a counter or table, or on the floor, with you sitting down next to it.

2. Ask your cat to "Shake," and reach out with your right hand, gently lifting your cat's right paw. Click your clicker once and immediately reward the cat with a treat. You should also say "Good Shake." Then let go of its paw. The cat will at first be

confused and perhaps a bit concerned about having its paws touched, so be very positive, and don't hold the paw for too long a period of time. Try to get the cat's attention focused onto the treat and off of its paw. Work this stage of the trick for at least a week before moving on.

Remember to teach your cat when it is hungry!

3. By this time your cat should begin realizing that the act of shaking seems to be producing food. Once the concern of having its feet touched has been replaced by anticipation of food, you can begin asking the cat to lift its paw on its own. Say "Shake," and move your right hand as if to lift the cat's right paw. Come very close, but do not actually pick it up. Hopefully your cat will lift its paw and meet your outstretched hand. If it does, take the cat's offered paw in your hand, click your clicker and reward the cat. Even if the cat just moves its paw a little bit, you should still reward it. If the cat is still not offering its paw on its own, try very gently tapping on the back side of the cat's lower leg with one finger while saying "Shake." This should encourage the cat to lift its paw. When it does, pick up the paw in your hand, click, and reward.

Once you have the cat shaking on command, you can teach it to shake with its left paw. Try using a different command for each paw, such as "Shake" for the right and "Give Me Five" for the left. Eventually, the cat will know which paw to raise by which command you give. Remember, do not overwork the cat, and always end on a positive note.

TRICK NO. 6

KISS

If you have sensitive skin, or are turned off by the thought of having meat baby food dabbed on your face or hand, then you may want to pass on this trick. Otherwise, the "Kiss" is a fun trick to teach your cat. Cats have much rougher tongues than dogs; it really is a unique feeling to have their little sandpaper tongues licking you.

Level of difficulty:

What you will need:
a clicker, gooey treats, and a helper

Length of session:
two to five minutes

Frequency of sessions:
once or twice every day

Advance preparation:
none

Previous trick required:
Sit

1. Decide on what treat you are going to use. Like the "Wash It" trick, you will need something gooey that can be dabbed on a helper's hand or face (yes, I said face). A piece of tuna or other tidbit won't work; it has to be viscous enough to stick for awhile. Try meat baby food, or the

gelatin from a
can of Spam.
When I have
to get a cat to
kiss an actor
on film, I usual-
ly use liver or
chicken-fla-
vored baby food
because it is
flesh-colored
and doesn't show
up on camera.

2. Place the cat on a table, in a sitting position. Have a helper sit directly in front of the cat, no more than a foot or two away. He or she should have the gooey treat already dabbed on face or hand. (Tell him or her that it's good for the skin!) You should have the clicker and a treat with you.

3. Allow the cat to see and smell the treat on your helper, then pull it back a foot or so. Hope that the cat is good and hungry!

4. Release the cat, say its name, and then say "Kiss." Most cats at this point will walk right over to your helper and begin licking the food off. If this happens, immediately click once and give the cat a different piece of food, perhaps a piece of cheese or tuna. If the cat does not walk over and begin licking off the food, try moving your helper closer and closer until you get the desired response. Practice this twice each day for several days before moving on.

5. Begin decreasing the amount of food dabbed on your helper, so that eventually there is no food at all, and the cat is simply responding to the verbal cue in expectation of the treat coming from you. This decrease should be done over a period of perhaps two weeks.

6. Begin increasing the distance between the cat and your helper, so that eventually the cat will travel across the room to deliver the kiss. Take your time doing this.

7. Of course, you should also teach your cat to kiss you. You might even teach it to kiss the family dog or another cat, if those pets are willing to sit there with food on their faces!

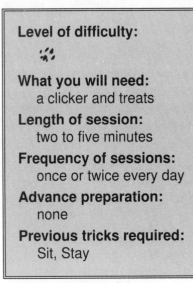

TRICK NO. 7

WAVE

I once did a commercial for a photocopy machine distributor. The producer wanted a cat to take a document to the copy machine, make a copy, and bring it back to the boss. The retrieve was easy; the actor just clipped the paper to the cat's collar. The boss then looks at the copy and the original, trying to determine which is which. The producer wanted the cat to point to the original document. I had my black-and-white cat Shadow do a "Sit/Stay" on the boss's desk, facing him. I stood off-camera behind the boss and asked Shadow to "Wave," which she promptly did. The boss was holding the papers up in front of himself; when Shadow waved, it appeared that she was choosing one of the papers.

Level of difficulty:

What you will need:
a clicker and treats

Length of session:
two to five minutes

Frequency of sessions:
once or twice every day

Advance preparation:
none

Previous tricks required:
Sit, Stay

"Wave" is an easy trick to teach, and most cats really love it. I have taught cats this trick in one session. In fact, some trainers don't like to teach their cats "Wave" because they often begin performing the trick on their own, with no cue at all. This can be a problem on the set; if a cat is supposed to be performing a "Sit/Stay" on a windowsill, for instance, and starts waving incessantly, the shot is ruined.

1. Ask the cat to "Sit" and "Stay" at the edge of a table. Make sure the cat is hungry, and let it see the treat in your hand.

2. Move the treat back and forth in front of the cat, just outside of its reach, and say "Wave." Make the treat as tempting as possible. If the cat is hungry, it will begin trying to figure out just how to get the treat from you. Make sure to  keep the treat at about face level. Eventually, the cat will try to grab your hand with its paw, or at least attempt to reach out to the treat. As soon as its paw reaches out toward you, click your clicker, give it the treat, and say "Good Wave." The cat shouldn't actually touch you; after all, you are teaching it to wave, not touch. You want it to eventually discriminate between the "Wave" and the "Shake." Attempt to keep the cat in a "Sit/Stay" position. If it breaks the sitting position, simply ask it to "Sit" again, and reward when it complies.

By this point, you should have a good feel for just how to manipulate the treat in just the right way to direct the cat's movement and keep its attention. Work this step for several days before moving on.

3. Once the cat is lifting its paw, you can slowly begin to increase your distance when you ask it to "Wave." Continue to move your "treat" hand in a tantalizing back-and-forth motion. This will eventually become the hand signal for "Wave." Keep practicing until the cat really gets it. Remember to always click the clicker and reward the cat when it does the right thing.

TRICK NO. 8
COME

One day I got a panicked call from a local producer. She needed a trained cat immediately, for a supermarket advertisement still shoot. Indy, my best worker, was outside amusing himself, completely out of sight. I went outside and at first called him verbally, to no avail. Then I got out my buzzer device and tried that. Indy came bolting out of the woods like a freight train. I rewarded him with some tuna and a hug. Then the two of us went off to do the commercial.

There is a scene in the movie *Homeward Bound* that shows the cat Sassy running up to Shadow, a golden

---

Level of difficulty:

🐾 🐾

What you will need:
  a sound-making device, treats, and a helper

Length of session:
  two to five minutes

Frequency of sessions:
  two to three times every day

Advance preparation:
  switch cat over to specific feeding times

Previous tricks required:

retriever, and hugging him. We actually had a remote control buzzer device built into the dog's collar, and a piece of
cooked liver clipped onto the dog's coat. The cat performed
perfectly; afterward, we rewarded the dog for his patience
and self-control with his own piece of liver.

The "Come" command is probably the most requested
behavior for a film-trained cat. You have seen it performed
many times without even realizing it; each time you see a cat
moving from one point to another, it is actually performing
the "Come."

Some of you may have already taught this trick to your
cats without knowing it. Owners will at dinnertime often
open up a can of cat food with an electric or manual can
opener; most cats will quickly learn that this sound means
that dinner is just a moment away. If the cat is hungry and
within hearing distance, it will most certainly come to you.
You have, without realizing it, taught your cat the "Come"
command.

I use a very similar method to teach my cats to "Come."
The first step involves putting my cats onto a specific feeding schedule (discussed in Part Two under "Creating the
Appropriate Environment"), so I can more easily predict
when they will be hungry. It is not absolutely necessary to
stop free-feeding, but you will have a better response if you
do. If you continue to free-feed, then choose a particular
time each day to feed your cat a special snack, perhaps a few
spoons of canned meat baby food or some tuna, or whatever
you find your cat to be crazy for.

The next step is deciding on what sound-making device
to use. I prefer to use a sound that is heard by the cat *only*
when you want it to "Come." It should not be a sound that

the cat would hear any other time in its daily routine. Your voice is heard by the cat all the time, so, though pleasant-sounding to the cat, it will not be unique or surprising enough to really get the cat's attention.

My sound-maker is a buzzer device that I put together myself from electrical parts available in most hardware or electronics stores. It consists of a nine-volt battery, a buzzer, a button switch, and a plastic housing that fits in my hand. It is about the size of a small television remote. I use the buzzer because it is a completely incongruous sound to a cat; they aren't likely to ever hear it anywhere else. Don't worry if you cannot construct a buzzer device; a referee's whistle, available at any sporting goods or toy store, will do just fine. Even a bicycle bell or squeak toy will work, if that's all you have. Just make sure that the sound you use is not so loud that it scares the cat. The *sound* the device makes is the actual call; you won't be saying "Come, Sasha." Make sure the cat hears the device at no time other than when you are calling it to you.

1. For two weeks, use your sound-making device once or twice as you are putting the cat's food bowl down. At no other time should the cat hear this sound. Then, let the cat eat undisturbed. Do not attempt to call your cat with the sound device yet. During this period, your cat will, just like Pavlov's dogs, be learning to associate the sound with the food. Eventually the cat will automatically understand that the sound means "I'm going to get to eat now." If you try the "Come" too soon, the conditioning may not be entirely in place, and you will compromise the trick.

2. After two weeks, you will be ready to try calling the cat to you with the sound-making device. You will need a helper to aid you at this stage. First, right at feeding time, put your cat in another room by itself or in a traveling crate and close the door. Next, prepare your cat's food and place it down in its normal spot. Then begin sounding your device; when your assistant hears this, he or she should open the door to release the cat. Continue intermittently sounding the device until your cat gets to the food. Then stop sounding the device, say "Good Come," and let the cat eat undisturbed.

If your cat does not "Come" well at this stage, it may not be hungry enough. Try going to specific feedings instead of free-feeding.

3. Once your cat is coming regularly to the food dish, you should try changing your location in the house. Go into the bedroom and sound the device; if your cat comes to you, give it a very special food

treat and praise it! If it goes to the normal feeding spot first, just be patient and keep sounding the device.

4. If your cat is an indoor/outdoor pet, begin trying the "Come" outside, at dinnertime. In this case the sound-making device needs to be loud enough for the cat to hear from a longer distance, so if you are using a whistle, blow a bit harder.

Keep in mind that this trick is dependent on your cat's food drive. As your cat becomes full, it will "Come" more slowly, with less reliability. You must stop the session before this occurs. Also, some cats are just more food-motivated than others. Let's hope your cat is one of these. Above all, always try to end on a positive note.

TRICK NO. 9
SPEAK

I once worked on a commercial that called for a white Persian to "Snuggle" in an older woman's lap. We easily got the shot. Then the director decided that he wanted to add a meow to the soundtrack. Unfortunately, the Persian was not trained to "Speak." Luckily I had brought Indy—who was practiced in this command—along as a back-up cat, something I have learned to always do as a precautionary measure. We simply took Indy into the recording studio, recorded him meowing, and dubbed it into the final version of the commercial.

Indy also came through for me as my only growling cat. I once had a baby bobcat that Indy wanted nothing to do with. The bobcat, however, *loved* Indy, and would

Level of difficulty:

What you will need:
a clicker and treats

Length of session:
two to five minutes

Frequency of sessions:
once or twice every day

Advance preparation:
prepare cat's dinner with an extra treat

Previous tricks required:

follow him around all day. Indy began growling at him to warn him off; I saw the opportunity when I was called by a producer who needed a soundtrack of a cat growling, and took both cats into the recording studio. We captured perfectly Indy's growling, and held onto the tape for future use.

It is possible that many of you already have cats that meow readily. For you, this trick will be easy. Some cats are more vocal than others, and will learn "Speak" much more quickly. Siamese cats are very vocal, for instance, and learn this trick easily. If your cat is fairly vocal, you shouldn't have much trouble.

This trick should be worked on right at feeding time. My cat Riley actually has to "Speak" for his dinner; it is a ritual with us, and he loves it. He comes up, sits right in front of me, and starts meowing away. If you always work the "Speak" as a prelude to feeding, you will actually be working the trick once or twice a day, every day, depending on how often you feed your cat. It will quickly become a happily anticipated routine to the cat.

1. Prepare the cat's dinner, and place an extra wonderful treat in it, perhaps a dollop of canned food or some tuna juice. With the cat at your feet in front of you, let it know you have its food. Then hold the food up at waist level and say the cat's name and then "Speak." You are actually going to tempt the cat with the food for a minute or so, and hope that you get it to vocalize. Any vocalization should be rewarded. If the cat does vocalize, immediately click your clicker, say "Good Speak," and feed it the food. Some cats will vocalize the first time, and others may take longer. You may have to shake the food around a bit, or move it in a tantalizing way.

2. Work Step One at feeding time every day. After you get the cat to vocalize regularly, you will want to "generalize" the behavior, or get the

cat to perform it in another area or time of day. Try it in a different room; have the cat sit in front of you, and with a treat in your hand say the cat's name and then "Speak." Eventually the cat will figure it out. Then try working the trick with the cat on a table, or even in your lap. If your cat does not respond well, end the session and try again later, perhaps at the next meal.

TRICK NO. 10
JUMP INTO LAP

I had to train a cat to do this trick for the film *Home for the Holidays*. Holly Hunter and the actress playing her mother (Anne Bancroft) were sitting at a table eating dinner; the shot called for a cat to jump up into Holly's lap and then onto the table, whereupon it would begin eating Holly's dinner. I used my cat Sasha for the part. I had prepped Sasha on this behavior for several weeks; she had gotten it down perfectly. Then when it came time to shoot the scene, director Jodie Foster decided that she wanted to start the scene with Sasha already up on the table eating off of a plate. Sasha never got to perform her trick. The name of the

Level of difficulty:

🐾 🐾

What you will need:
a clicker, treats, and a helper

Length of session:
two to five minutes

Frequency of sessions:
once or twice every day

Advance preparation:
none

Previous trick required:
Come

game in show business is flexibility, though, and Sasha performed the new scene easily. Unfortunately, she now thinks it's okay to jump up onto the dinner table and share food with me!

As you may have suspected, this is an easy trick to teach. On command, the cat has to simply jump into someone's lap. You will need a helper (and his or her lap) for this one, because ultimately your cat should be trained to jump into someone's lap on your command. You can teach it just to jump into yours, but that's not as challenging. Make sure your helper is not wearing shorts for this one.

1. Have a helper sit in a chair. He or she should have the clicker in one hand and a treat in the other. Make sure your helper makes it obvious to the cat that he or she has the treat.

2. Position yourself about two or three feet from your helper while holding the cat with its feet on the ground. Then, have your helper click the clicker about five or six times, very rapidly, as a way to get the cat's attention. At the same time, you should say "Jump" to the cat.

3. Let go of your cat as soon as you hear the clicker. Most cats, if hungry, will jump up into the helper's lap to get the treat. He or she should then immediately click once and reward the cat. If the cat does not jump into your helper's lap, it may be necessary to start with the cat closer to the helper, or even in the helper's lap, if only to acquaint them both and let the cat know where the best place to be is.

4. After you have the cat performing the "Jump" from two or three feet away, begin gradually increasing the distance until you can reliably get the cat to cross the room and jump up into the helper's lap.

5. If you have perfected this, you may want to teach the cat to jump up onto someone's shoulders. Use the same methods, and change only the location of the treat.

Don't forget to have fun with your cat!

TRICK NO. 11
RUB IT

In the movie *Home for the Holidays*, my cat Tigger worked as a double for my other cat, Sasha. Sasha is a great worker, but she isn't a great rubber. Tigger is, though, and he looks a lot like Sasha, so when a shot called for a cat to perform a "Rub It" I just substituted Tigger. He loves being affectionate and close.

This could be one of the easier tricks to teach your cat, who probably rubs up against you already, without being asked to. Cats are affectionate animals, and love to make physical contact with their owners. Some behaviorists also think that cats rub up against things as a way of marking territory.

The object of "Rub It" is to get the cat to

Level of difficulty:

What you will need:
a clicker, treats, and a helper

Length of session:
three to five minutes

Frequency of sessions:
once or twice every day

Advance preparation:
none

Previous tricks required:

rub up against you or another person on command. Again, some cats are less sociable than others, and may not be too open to the idea of rubbing up against someone other than yourself. If that is the case, you can just teach the cat to rub against you.

1. Have a helper standing or sitting on the edge of a chair. You should have the reward and the clicker.

2. Place the cat two or three feet in front of the helper, and then release it. Many cats at this point will instinctively walk over to the helper and rub up against him or her. If you are lucky enough to have this occur, by all means, click and

reward. If not, you will have to use food guidance to get the cat to "accidentally" rub up against your helper. Say the cat's name and then "Rub It," and then bait the cat with the treat, leading it right past the helper's leg, making contact as it goes by. If this occurs, immediately click and reward. You may have to get the helper to slowly and unobtrusively move his or her leg slightly to get it into the right position.

3. Once the cat actually rubs up against your helper on cue, it is time for you to begin slowly backing away, removing yourself bit by bit from the situation. The objective is to be able to send the cat at least a few feet toward the

helper and have it rub up against his or her leg. You still must return to give the reward, however. Do not have the helper give the reward; the cat will just go right for the treat and forget about rubbing up.

4. If you are able to get this far, then try teaching the cat to rub up against an inanimate object such as a table or sofa, using the same treat-guiding technique. Also, remember to begin teaching the trick in different rooms; if you stick to just one room, chances are the cat will only perform the trick there.

Change the type of treats you use once each week!

TRICK NO. 12
PLAY BALL

I was once hired to work on a commercial for Washington State Natural Gas. The producer wanted to show a house cat lazily batting at a table tennis ball floating in midair, supposedly held aloft on a cushion of warm air rising from a floor heat vent. The ball was in actuality supported top and bottom by thin fishing line; all I needed to do was to train my cat Riley to bat at the ball while it was being manipulated up and down by the props person. Riley quickly learned to bat at the ball, but kept getting his claws stuck in the fishing line. Fortunately, we managed to get the shot before Riley finally snapped the line, grabbed the ball, and ran off with it.

Level of difficulty:

What you will need:
a clicker, treats, and a ball (or any toy the cat loves)

Length of session:
three to five minutes

Frequency of sessions:
once every day

Advance preparation:
none

Previous tricks required:

Though this is not a difficult trick to teach, your success with the "Play Ball" trick will depend largely on the temperament of your cat. Cats with a particularly high prey or stalking drive should do quite well, as should cats that just love to run around and stick their noses into everything. If your cat is active and feisty and loves toys, then you shouldn't have much of a problem. However, if your cat is a very low-key, laid-back animal that tends not to become all that excited, you may have some difficulty motivating it to perform this trick.

1. Choose a toy that your cat loves to play with and stalk. A ball made of cloth, yarn, or rubber—or even a crumpled-up wad of newspaper—will do nicely. Size and texture are not too important; unlike the "Fetch" trick, which requires the cat to actually pick the toy up in its mouth, the "Play Ball" trick requires only that the cat bat the toy around with its paws. A three- to four-inch diameter ball should work perfectly. Do not use a ball or toy with catnip in it, as this will cause the cat to lose focus and become "spacey."

2. With the cat in front of you, tease it with the ball for a few seconds until it becomes very excited. Roll the ball quickly from hand to

hand, perhaps also bouncing it a bit, until the cat begins to paw or swat at it. Then roll the ball at the cat and say "Play Ball." As soon as the cat bats at the ball with its paw, click and reward. Continue working this step until the cat begins to understand that whenever it swats at the ball, it gets a treat.

3. Slowly begin to increase your distance from the cat; continue rolling the ball at it while giving the command "Play Ball," and encourage it to bat it around on its own. Begin to then delay the click and reward somewhat, so that the cat begins playing with the ball for longer periods of time. Eventually you should be able to roll the ball to the cat, say "Play Ball," and let the cat go at it by itself for twenty to thirty seconds before clicking and rewarding. Through the teaching of this trick, remain upbeat, and convince the cat that the ball is the most fun, desirable item this side of a live mouse. As the cat becomes good at it, try to involve yourself in the game; you might even eventually teach the cat to bat the ball to you, sparking a game of catch!

TRICK NO. 13
STAY

During the filming of the movie *Homeward Bound*, one scene required that a cat sit and watch several dogs running off into the distance. In actuality, we had placed the cat in a "Sit" and "Stay" (henceforth called a "Sit/Stay") position. Almost every still photo session involving a cat requires me to use the "Stay" command. Photographers almost never want a cat moving, but rather in a "Sit/Stay," "Stand/Stay," or "Down/Stay." The "Stay" command is invaluable to me; I could not run my business without it.

I once was required to train a cat to appear to be pulling a dogsled in the snow. Fortunately, it was a still photograph and not film or tape; this meant that I could set it up so that it simply

Level of difficulty:

What you will need:
a clicker and treats

Length of session:
two to three minutes

Frequency of sessions:
two or three times every day

Advance preparation:
none

Previous trick required:
Sit

appeared as if the cat were pulling a sled. We shot the scene in a studio with a backdrop and fake snow, which meant not having to take cats into cold, snowy weather, which they despise. I chose to use my cat Indy, who was very coopera- tive and would allow me to place him in just about any situa- tion or position without worrying. I taught Indy to do a "Stand/Stay" while wearing a special harness; from there it was just a matter of taking Indy to the studio and hooking his harness up to a dogsled for the shot. The shot turned out so well I used it in my own advertising.

Once your cat has mastered the "Sit" command, you can move on to the "Stay." "Stay" means that whatever posi- tion the cat is in, it must remain there until released with the word "Okay." I recommend you begin with the cat in a sitting position; the "Stay" requires the cat to be focused, and the sitting position helps focus the cat.

I utilize natural cat language to teach a cat to "Stay." When two cats are interacting and one does not want the other to come any closer, it will tap the approaching cat on the forehead with its paw, then hiss. The other cat under- stands this to mean "you are coming into my space, and I do not approve." Remember that felines are highly territorial, and covet their own space. The cat that is touched on the head will usually respond by staying put, right where it is, until it has figured out an appropriate way of backing off without losing face. I mimic this natural behavior to teach my cats to "Stay," instead of using leash restraint, which can panic a cat and lead to a lack of trust and desire to learn. Make sure there are no distractions occurring. Even street noise or a television left on in another room will disturb the cat's concentration.

1. First ask your cat to "Sit" on a table in front of you. Cats like to be up high; yours will be happier up on a table as opposed to the floor. Make sure the cat is *away* from the edge of the table. If the cat is at the edge, it has no option but to stay where it is; it will not have learned the concept from you.

2. Once your cat is sitting, put one or two fingers on its forehead and say "psssst" and then "Stay." Do not say "psssst" too loudly, or it may frighten the cat. You are simply alerting the cat that you want it to respect your space. It will instinctively understand this. Most cats will stay right where they are for at least a few seconds. You should reward the cat for even a second of nonmovement.

3. After any positive response, reward the cat with a treat and praise. If your cat did not "Stay," try saying "psssst" louder, until you get the desired response.

4. With practice, you should be able to begin gradually moving away from your cat while it is in the "Sit/Stay" position.

Eventually you should be able to get all the way across the room without your cat moving. Getting to this point will probably take several days. Be patient, and regularly return to praise your cat.

5. Once the cat is reliably staying where you want it to, you should replace the "psssst" with just the word "Stay."

6. As you get farther away from the cat you will no longer be able to touch it on its forehead. You should continue making the gesture, however; first from a few inches from the cat's head, then a foot, then a few feet, and so forth. This eventually becomes the hand signal for "Stay." Cats respond to hand signals as well as or better than verbal commands because body posture among animals is a key form of communication. Your ultimate goal should be getting your cat to "Stay" from across the room, using only the verbal "Stay" and the hand signal. The real test comes if the cat responds to a "Stay" command while it is in motion. If at any time the cat moves during the "Stay," simply walk back to it, touch it on the head and say "pssst." Then slowly walk away.

7. Practice the "Stay" command at least two to three times each day, and remember to release it from the session with the word "Okay."

8. Once you have perfected this trick, slowly begin introducing distractions, one at a time. A friend walking past the cat, or your opening and closing the front door will suffice. Eventually, your cat should "Stay" while a herd of elephants troop by (if your cat can do this I certainly have a job for it).

A word about using treats to reward "Stay." Your cat might be too food-motivated to "Stay" in one spot if it senses food. If this is the case, try using no treats at first, only praise. Also try working the "Stay" after feeding time, not before. The "Stay" may be the only trick that requires this technique. After a meal, your cat will be more sedate, and more willing to "Stay" in one spot.

Trick No. 14
RISE

"Rise" is a fun and relatively easy trick to teach. The objective is to get the cat to balance itself up on its hind quarters, with its front paws off the ground and tucked in, as if begging. Most cats will pick it up rather quickly. Cats that are pudgy or wide in the hips may have an easier time learning this trick than skinny, long-bodied cats, because of their lower center of gravity, which affects the animal's ability to balance itself on its rear haunches. Even thin cats can eventually master it, though, so don't worry. It will just take a bit longer.

Level of difficulty:

What you will need:
a clicker and treats

Length of session:
three to five minutes

Frequency of sessions:
once or twice every day

Advance preparation:
none

Previous trick required:
Sit

1. Start with your cat in a "Sit" position. Let your cat see and smell that you have a treat in your hand. Then ask the cat to "Rise"

while moving the treat two or three inches *directly* above the cat's head, so that the easiest way for the cat to get at it is to sit up on its haunches. Make sure you do not hold the treat up too high, as this will encourage the cat to stand up on its hind legs, not rear back on its haunches. By this time, though, you probably have developed a real feel for manipulating the treat in just the right way; you should know exactly how close to place it to get your cat to respond in the desired fashion. At this point the best training technique will be found through trial and error, so be patient and positive, and know when to take a break.

2. As soon as the cat rises up into the "Rise" position, click your clicker, reward it,

and say "Good Rise." Do not let the cat reach up with its front paws to try and grab the treat out of your hand. If it tries this, remove the treat and start again. Make sure your timing is just right; the moment the cat is in the "Rise" position, click

and reward. Ideally, the cat's front paws should be in a relaxed position in front of its body. Work this step several times each day before moving on.

3. Over time, begin to back away from the cat when you give the verbal command "Rise." Also, continue using the raising-up motion of your hand with the treat in it; this will become the hand signal for "Rise."

TRICK NO. 15
DOWN

A while back I worked on a commercial for the Washington State Lottery Commission, starring Richard Moll ("Bull" from *Night Court*). The producers wanted to push the "Fat Cat" theme, and needed to have a cat lying on a big pillow smoking a fat cigar. I approached the trick in several steps. First, I trained my cat Indy to master a "Down/Stay" on the pillow provided with one of his front legs tucked in underneath his body. Then I had the props department make a fake, life-sized cat paw holding a dummy cigar, which had a special compartment at the end to hold some tuna. I trained Indy to mouth the end of the cigar by placing a choice piece of tuna on the tip. With lots of repetition, he learned to reliably

Level of difficulty:

What you will need:
a clicker and treats

Length of session:
two to five minutes

Frequency of sessions:
two or three times every day

Advance preparation:
none

Previous trick required:
Sit

place his mouth on the tip of the cigar whenever it was offered, whether or not the tuna was present. The fake paw was introduced into the scene from the lower left, making it appear to be his own, which was in fact tucked beneath him, out of sight. With the aid of some good camera work and just the right angle, we got the shot of him puffing on the cigar. The cat was ultimately so content that he purred through the whole filming. You can even hear it on the finished commercial!

Teaching the "Down" command will require some patience on your part. It will certainly take longer to teach than the "Sit" command. From a cat's point of view, "Down" might be viewed as a vulnerable position to be in; it must therefore be assured that nothing unusual or threatening will occur during the exercise. Above all, cats value their safety and must be assured of this before any learning can occur. Remember, as with all the tricks, to begin working this one with absolutely no distractions present.

1. Place your cat atop a table or dresser and ask it to "Sit." This time, unlike when teaching "Sit," you want the cat to be *at the edge.*

2. Hold the treat a few inches in front of your cat's nose. Make sure the cat is focused on the treat but can't reach it with its mouth.

3. Slowly move the treat straight down until it is a few inches *below* the surface of the table or dresser. As you begin this movement, say the cat's name and then "Down." The cat should eventually follow the treat down and go into a crouching posture. Do not click

at this point. You won't click until the full "Down" position is attained in Step Four. Learn to move the treat at just the right speed so that the cat's attention remains on it.

4. Once the cat has mastered Step Three, you will want to begin helping it into a full "Down" position. With the cat in a crouching position and the treat just below the surface of the table, take your free hand, place it on the cat's shoulders, and apply some gentle pressure downward. Gently rock the cat's shoulders from side to side; eventually (if you have conditioned the cat to accept this level of handling), the cat should extend its front paws out in front. Remember to keep your cat focused on the treat and not your hand on its back. You may have to adjust the distance of the treat from the cat's nose accordingly. When the cat stretches its paws out fully, click your clicker, say "Good Down," and give it the treat. It is important not to force the issue here; take several days if necessary to achieve this complete "Down." If your cat isn't fond of being handled a lot, you may have to settle for the crouching position instead of the full "Down." Simply say "Okay" to release the cat and end the session.

5. You may want to keep your hand resting on the cat's shoulders at this stage, to maintain the position. Make the cat think that you are petting its shoulders and neck. Don't pet the cat on the rump, however, as this will cause the cat to stand up.

6. Finally, tell the cat to "Stay" and then slowly step back. Use the same pointing gesture you did for the "Sit/Stay," in combination with the spoken "Down" command. Praise the cat if it keeps the position. Once you feel confident that the cat will stay in position, gradually begin increasing your distance from the cat after giving the command. Eventually, you should be able to cross the room and return without the cat breaking its position. When you want to release the cat, simply say "Okay," then give it a pet.

Trick No. 16
Wash It

I had attempted to use this trick during the shooting of *The Good Son*, starring Macaulay Culkin and Elijah Wood. The scene had Macaulay and Elijah playing with a homemade gun that shot out metal bolts; they see a cat sitting on a stone fence leisurely washing itself, and decide to shoot at it.

Level of difficulty:

What you will need:
a clicker, a cotton swab, regular treats, and some gooey treats

Length of session:
three to five minutes

Frequency of sessions:
once every day

Advance preparation:
none

Previous tricks required:
Sit, Stay

I used my cat Shadow, who usually performs the "Wash It" perfectly, even with me several yards away. Of course, this time Shadow decided to ignore my "Wash It" command, choosing instead to sit there and watch all the activity in the background. The prop department set up a very thin guyline that went from the gun to a tree right next to the cat, and had the projectile follow this wire right to the tree. Though we couldn't get Shadow to perform the trick, we did manage to get a shot that showed Shadow momentarily stop what she was doing, look at the tree, then run off. In real life she was running to me; I was buzzing the "Come" buzzer and holding a spoonful of food.

This was a particularly hard shot to set up because of the myriad of distractions present. We were near the ocean, with large waves crashing in every few seconds. It was also windy, and dozens of noisy seagulls were milling about. The set was crowded with actors and crew members. To make matters worse, there were train tracks only about fifty yards away. A train would noisily pass by every twenty minutes. All these distractions made it nearly impossible to get Shadow to perform.

You will need a particularly gooey treat for this one. I use strained-meat baby food or the oil from canned tuna. The treat has to be one that you can apply to the cat's front foreleg and have remain there for a while, at least long enough for the cat to get some good licks in. If you tried to use a piece of tuna or cheese, it just wouldn't stay put long enough. Chicken fat or butter may also tempt your feline.

1. Start with your cat in a "Sit/Stay" position on a table. Then, using a cotton swab as an applicator, quickly smear some of the gooey treat on one of the cat's front forelegs. Do not put any on the cat's paws; a cat

usually will try to shake it off the paw rather than lick it off. At first, your cat may be confused and a bit resistant; this will quickly pass, though, when it realizes how good this foreign substance on its foreleg tastes.

2. Immediately after you have smeared the food on the cat's foreleg, say "Wash It," while you also mimic licking your own hand. This will be the hand signal for the trick. Once this is done, just wait. Eventually the cat's nose will locate the

food on its foreleg. The instant the cat lifts its paw and starts cleaning itself, click your clicker once and give a reward from your hand. You can use the same food that is smeared on the cat. Also, verbally praise the cat by saying "Good Wash It."

3. Repeat this trick two or three sessions each day. If you want to extend the time that the cat is actually cleaning itself, then just delay the click and reward.

4. Once the cat knows what it is you are asking, begin to reduce the amount of food you smear on the cat. Try just dabbing on a tiny amount of tuna juice (the oil variety) with a cotton swab. Eventually you should be able to completely eliminate the food, and get the cat to wash itself just by giving the verbal cue, the hand signal, and the reward.

TRICK NO. 17
OVER

During the filming of *Homeward Bound,* we were required to teach a cat to jump out of a garbage dumpster and run down an alley. While the head cat trainer on the set, Tammy Maples, was down the alley with a buzzer and treats, waiting for the "action" cue, I was, you guessed it, *in* the dumpster holding the cat Sassy, waiting to hear the buzzer. When it finally sounded, I let go of Sassy; she jumped out perfectly and ran down the alley to Tammy, who had a nice spoonful of meat baby food waiting. I eventually jumped out of the dumpster too, and went home to take a long hot shower, but

Level of difficulty:

What you will need:
treats, a hurdle, a sound-making device, and a helper

Length of session:
three to five minutes

Frequency of sessions:
once every day

Advance preparation:
make or purchase hurdle; set it up in a quiet room

Previous trick required:
Come

not before the crew got some great pictures of me in the dumpster. And they say that show business is glamorous.

The objective of this trick is to teach your cat to jump over some type of obstacle. You can usually obtain some type of hurdle jump from a pet store that sells agility equipment for use with dogs. If you are not able to find this, you can make something yourself. Try using a board that is less than an inch thick, about one foot high, and about five feet long; mount it lengthwise onto another board. Whatever you use, the top of the jump should be relatively thin, to prevent the cat from jumping up *onto* it instead of jumping *over* it. It should also be long enough to prevent the cat from walking around instead of going over.

1. Set the jump up in a quiet room. Have a seated or crouching helper hold the cat on one side of the jump. Position yourself on the other side.

2. Have your helper release the cat just as you sound your sound-making device. Also say the cat's name and "Over." In actuality, you are asking the cat to come to you over a jump.

At first, you may have to bait the cat over the jump with a treat. Be patient; the first jump is the hardest to get.

3. Once the cat is reliably jumping over, begin increasing the distances from the jump for both you and the cat. You can also begin raising the height of the jump.

4. Try moving on to other obstacles, such as piles of books, laundry baskets, coffee tables, or what have you.

TRICK NO. 18
CLIMB A LADDER

Teaching a cat to climb a stepladder is not as hard as it sounds. Because cats are very agile animals, a ladder is really child's play to them. The trick is set up so that the cat will simply climb to the top of a stepladder (see photo). I use a ladder with three steps and a top platform. You can use any short ladder you have.

Level of difficulty:

What you will need:
a clicker, a sound-making device, treats, a stepladder, and a helper

Length of session:
three to five minutes

Frequency of sessions:
once or twice every day

Advance preparation:
set up short ladder in a quiet room

Previous trick required:
Come

1. Set the ladder up in a quiet place, then place the cat at the foot of it. You may want to have a helper hold the cat at first, then release it at the appropriate time.

2. Standing next to the ladder, use your sound-making device to call the cat to you, up the ladder. Also, say the cat's name and then the command "Climb." You may have to actually reach over the ladder at first to get the cat to come directly up instead of going around. You may also have to bait the cat up the

steps at first with a treat. The cat is actually performing the "Come" trick, albeit up a ladder. If it does come up the ladder to the top platform, reward. Have patience; it may take a while to get the first positive response.

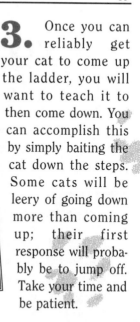

3. Once you can reliably get your cat to come up the ladder, you will want to teach it to then come down. You can accomplish this by simply baiting the cat down the steps. Some cats will be leery of going down more than coming up; their first response will probably be to jump off. Take your time and be patient.

4. Once the cat is performing the trick well, you can increase the length of the ladder.

Trick No. 19
Balance Beam

Once you have the cat confidently climbing up and down a ladder, you can move on to the "Balance Beam" trick.

1. Set up two stepladders about three to four feet from each other, then place a sturdy wooden board of about four inches in width between them, bridging the ladders from top to top (see photo). Have the cat perform the "Climb a Ladder" and then use your noise-making device to call the cat to you across the platform. Bait the cat across, if necessary.

Then have the cat climb down the other side of the ladder to the floor.

2. Once the cat has mastered this, reduce the width of the board to two inches. Again, at this stage, you want to make sure that the apparatus is stable and secure; if it shakes

or wavers, it may put off the cat completely. Remember, cats won't do anything they don't want to do. It is your responsibility to create a positive environment for the cat.

3. Once the cat is reliably crossing the two-inch-wide board, you may want to try going to a one-inch-wide board. The cat is certainly agile enough to do it; just make sure the board you choose is stable.

TRICK NO. 20
THROUGH A HOOP

I once had to set up a shot for a greeting card that required a picture of a cat jumping through a flaming hoop. My fearless cat Riley is very adept at jumping through hoops, so I thought I'd give him a try. When the hoop was lighted, the flames were only about an inch or two high, and came nowhere near Riley, who was very comfortable with the trick and performed it repeatedly. (*I don't recommend you try this flaming trick, for the safety of you, your cat, and your home.*)

The objective of this trick is to teach

Level of difficulty:

What you will need:
a clicker, a sound-making device, treats, a hoop with mounting stand, two low footstools or pedestals, and a helper

Length of session:
two to five minutes

Frequency of sessions:
once or twice every day

Advance preparation:
purchase or build a hoop with stand; set it up between pedestals

Previous tricks required:
Sit, Stay, and Come

your cat to jump through a hoop from one platform to another. Cats are extremely agile, and most should be able to learn this trick fairly quickly, especially those who are confident, curious, and food-motivated.

You will need to purchase or build a hoop with some sort of stand; some pet shops may have them, or you can improvise with materials purchased in a toy store. You can even use a small hula hoop. The hoop you use should be about two feet in diameter and of a bright color so it is easily visible. You will also need two small stools or pedestals of equal height to place on each side of the hoop; the cat will jump from one, go through the hoop, and land on the other. These stools or pedestals should be carpeted so that your cat feels sure-footed on them. These pedestals should also be stable; any shakiness may upset the cat and send it packing.

1. Mount the hoop on both sides so that it is stable and secure. If the hoop did not come with metal mounting stands, then attach it to two chairs using secure straps or tape. The bottom section of the hoop should be at first no more than four inches higher than the surfaces of the flanking pedestals, so that the cat needn't jump too high to get through on the first try. Set up the pedestals so that they flank the hoop. Each pedestal should be no more than six inches away from the hoop.

2. Have a helper place the cat on one of the pedestals, facing the hoop. Place yourself on the other side of the hoop, behind that pedestal, facing the cat.

3. Bait the cat through the hoop with a favorite treat, while saying the cat's name and then "Through." You will probably have to reach over and let the cat smell the treat, then gradually withdraw it through the hoop. If the cat is hungry, it will eventually figure out how to get to the treat. Be patient; it may take a few minutes, but it will happen. When the cat jumps

through the hoop and onto the pedestal on your side of the hoop, immediately click once and reward. Work this stage of the trick for several days, or until the cat is reliably jumping through the hoop.

You can also try using your sound-making device to get your cat to "Come" to you through the hoop.

4. Gradually begin raising the hoop and lengthening the distance between the pedestals. Within a few weeks you should have your cat jumping appreciable distances on cue.

TRICK No. 21
THROUGH A TUNNEL

You can purchase a tunnel in almost any toy or pet store, or you can use the inner cardboard cylinder found inside carpet rolls, as long as it is wide enough for the cat to fit through. Vent hosing for a clothes dryer might also work, provided it is wide enough to comfortably let the cat pass through.

Some timid cats may not want to go into a tunnel. Do not force them to; stick to the "Through a Hoop" trick instead. Other cats, however, will have no problem, especially if they have a high food drive and a good level of curiosity.

Level of difficulty:

What you will need:
a sound-making device, treats, a travel crate, and a short tunnel

Length of session:
three to four minutes

Frequency of sessions:
once or twice every day

Advance preparation:
set up tunnel with travel crate at its mouth

Previous tricks required:
Sit, Stay, Come, and Through a Hoop

1. Have a helper hold the cat at one end of the tunnel. He or she can also have the cat in its carrying crate right at the mouth of the tunnel. You should be at the other end, with your whistle or buzzer and a great treat.

2. Have your helper release the cat or open the crate door. At the same time, you should whistle or buzz for the cat to come to you through the tunnel. If it does, reward it. That is really all it is: simply a "Come" through the tunnel. Because your cat already knows the "Come" command, this shouldn't be too hard, unless your cat is extremely timid. In any case, just make sure your cat is hungry.

3. Gradually lengthen the tunnel. With practice, you may be able to forego the need for a helper; simply put the cat into a "Sit/Stay" position at the mouth of the tunnel, go to the other end, and call it.

TRICK NO. 22
RING IT

Those who teach their cats to ring a bell do so usually because they want the cats to have a way of telling them when they are hungry or when they want to go out or come in. This can be cute, but it can also be annoying if the cat is a smart one. Many figure out that they can train their owners to pull out the food or open the back door just by ringing that darned bell. If you decide to teach "Ring It," just make sure your cat doesn't eventually let it get out of hand by ringing the bell at all hours!

Teaching this trick will be easier if you have already taught your cat the "Sit," "Stay," and, especially, the "Wave" commands, as this exact foot movement will be needed for it to ring the bell.

Level of difficulty:

What you will need:
a clicker, treats, and a bell

Length of session:
three to five minutes

Frequency of sessions:
once every day

Advance preparation:
mount or hang bell above table

Previous tricks required:
Sit, Stay, and Wave

1. Obtain a bell in a toy store, pet shop, or marine supply store. If you are using a small bell, hang it from a thin string or ribbon so that it is suspended about ten to twelve inches above the surface of the table you work your cat on. You might try hanging the bell from a tall table lamp or thumb-tacking it to the wall. If you are using a larger bell purchased at a marine supply store, mount it on a wooden stand with the mounting hardware provided. Make sure its clapper is six to ten inches above the surface of the table; position it too low or high and the cat may lose interest.

2. Place your cat into a "Sit/Stay" on the table, in a spot where it can easily reach the dangling bell. The cat should be facing you, with the bell in between.

3. Ask your cat to "Wave." Hold the treat directly behind the bell, and try to tantalize the cat into touching the treat with its paw. The longer you can extend the time of the "Wave," the better. You should have a good feel for treat manipulation by now, so use this skill to really focus your cat's attention. The object here is to get the cat to accidentally touch the string or the bell (or the clapper on the marine bell), causing it to ring.

4. If the cat makes contact with the string or the bell, even if it doesn't ring, click once and reward. Eventually you will get the cat to ring the bell on a regular basis. Work this step for several sessions each day, until the cat begins to understand that ringing the bell gets it a nice treat. This is textbook "conditioned response."

5. Once the cat understands that ringing the bell gets it a treat, substitute the command "Ring It" for "Wave." You have in effect used one established behavior (waving) to facilitate another (ringing a bell). This is called "chaining."

6. Now begin slowly increasing the distance between you and the cat. The objective here is to get the cat to ring the bell on command with you farther and farther away, until you are across the room.

7. Next, move the bell to where you will want to use it on a daily basis. Many owners will suspend the bell somewhere close to the back door, either inside or out, so that the cat can alert the owner to its desire to go out or come in. You can even have one bell inside and one outside. Work the "Ring It" in this new location, with click and reward, until the cat gets comfortable with it. Because of the new location, you may have to back up a few steps. Now, in addition to getting a treat, the cat may also get let into the house. For those that do not let their cats outside, an alternative is to place the bell in the kitchen, so that the cat can "Ring It" when it wants to eat. Make sure this does not get out of hand, though, and lead to obesity and an ever-ringing bell.

Trick No. 23
Go With

The goal of this cute trick is to get your cat to follow along with someone as he or she walks down a hall or around a room. To teach it, your cat will need to be conditioned to the clicker, and have a reasonably high food drive. Though this is not an extremely difficult trick to teach, cats with a low food drive may not respond as quickly as cats that love to chow down. For this reason, I recommend that you go to a regular feeding schedule instead of free-feeding (if you haven't already). You will also need treats, the services of a helper, and a travel crate.

Level of difficulty:

What you will need:
a clicker, a helper, treats, and a travel crate

Length of session:
five minutes

Frequency of sessions:
once every day

Advance preparation:
none

Previous trick required:
Come

1. Start working this trick in a hallway, to ensure that the cat can only move

either toward you or away from you, with no chance of any
significant lateral movement. This will help focus
the cat's attention.
Position yourself
at one end of the
hallway with the
cat at your feet in
its travel crate
(alternatively, you
can hold the cat if
a crate is not avail-
able). Have your
helper stand about
one or two feet in
front of the cat, with
his or her back to

you. Your helper should have the clicker in one hand. He or
she should also be holding a treat in one hand; at the start,
it should be held low enough so that the cat is tempted by it.
Make sure the cat is aware of the treat before you open the
crate (or physically
release it).

2. Release the
cat while
saying "Go With" to
the cat. At the same
time, have your
helper click the
clicker repeatedly
while slowly begin-

ning to walk down the hallway. He or she should make sure that the treat is prominently displayed low enough to attract the cat's attention. Hopefully, if the cat is hungry, it will begin to follow the helper down the hall. If it doesn't, chances are it isn't hungry enough or isn't aware of the treat. Continue to work at this step until you can get your cat to reliably follow your helper down the hall while he or she brandishes the treat and continues to click the whole way. Make sure the cat gets its well-deserved treat at the end of the hall.

3. Gradually have your helper reduce the amount of clicking; eventually he or she should be clicking only two or three times at the beginning and two or three times at the end. The helper should also not hold the treat down as low each time; the goal is to teach the cat to follow the helper closely, all the way down the hall, then get the treat reward.

4. Once the cat is regularly performing the "Go With" command in this fashion, try giving the cat the command when it is not in the crate or being held. The helper should still click at the beginning and end, and reward the animal with a treat at the end of the hall.

5. Begin working the trick in different areas of the home, perhaps the living room or bedroom. It may take the cat a few sessions to get used to this; the freedom to move laterally may at first be a distraction. Be patient, and remember not to overwork the cat. There's no rush!

6. If you allow your cat to go outside, try performing this trick in the yard, with as few distractions as possible. Or, continue to work it inside with a gradual introduction of distractions, perhaps a radio or television turned on, or some random items strewn on the floor.

TRICK No. 24

COME MARK

Actors have to situate themselves on a specific spot, or "mark," when getting ready to play a scene, so that the cameras can be properly focused and so that the scene itself can

<table>
<tr><td>

Level of difficulty:

🐾 🐾 🐾

What you will need:
a clicker, treats, a six-inch-square carpet (or wood) "mark," and a helper

Length of session:
three minutes

Frequency of sessions:
once or twice every day

Advance preparation:
none

Previous tricks required:
Come and Stay

</td></tr>
</table>

be physically structured to fit the upcoming action. Animal actors also need to learn to come to a mark. On the film set I try to let the environment determine what the cat's mark will be. During the outdoor shooting of *Homeward Bound*, we used large rocks or pieces of tree bark (we called them "bark marks"). If I were to do a scene in a home, on a sofa or bed, I would use a book, a pillow, a magazine, or even a dirty sock. The mark, in other words, is usually something that blends into the environment, and does not look contrived or obvious to the viewer.

It is not hard to teach this trick, but your cat will first need to know "Come" and "Stay" before you can begin. This is another trick that will necessitate the use of a helper.

1. Obtain a six-inch-square piece of carpet or wood that is of a different color and texture than the flooring of the room used to teach the trick. This will be the cat's "mark." If it is made of wood, make sure there are no splinters or rough edges for the cat to hurt itself on.

2. Place this mark about one foot in front of you. You should be in a sitting or squatting position or on your knees. Have a helper hold the cat at a distance of about four feet away from the mark. Have the food treat in one hand and the clicker in the other, and let the cat see the treat.

3. Have your helper release the cat. At the same time say "Come Mark" and then click your clicker four to six times. (Don't use one click; that means "job well done." You use the

repeated clicks here just as an attention-getter, much the way the buzzer or whistle would be used. Don't actually use the buzzer or whistle, though, as this should only mean "Come.") The cat's natural reaction will be to start coming toward you. If it does this, it will have to walk over the mark to get to you and the food. The second the cat steps on the mark with both front feet, click your clicker once and give it the treat.

4. Your cat may try to go around the mark to get to you and the food. If this happens, use the treat to lure the cat right to the mark. Hold the treat inches from your cat's nose, if need be. When your cat steps  on the mark, click and reward. If the cat steps on, then overruns, the mark, you can either stop it with a treat or touch it on the head and say "pssst." Release the cat from the session with the word "Okay," and let it rest for a while.

5. Once you have the cat reliably coming to its mark, begin asking it to "Stay," then *slowly* increase your distance from the mark. Praise the cat if it stays. Get it used to being on the mark with you several feet away.

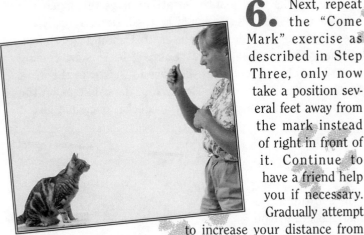

6. Next, repeat the "Come Mark" exercise as described in Step Three, only now take a position several feet away from the mark instead of right in front of it. Continue to have a friend help you if necessary. Gradually attempt to increase your distance from the mark. Also, gradually increase the cat's distance from the mark. Be patient, and do not overwork the cat.

7. Once you can get your cat to go to a mark reliably, with you stationed six feet away, gradually decrease the size of the mark itself, until it is only about two or three inches square. Take *at least* two weeks to do this. You can also train the cat to go to a different type of mark—for instance, a book or a pillow. If you choose to do this, however, you will need to retrain the cat to this new mark, from Step Two on.

Remember: Quiet on the set!

TRICK NO. 25
PLAY DEAD

This trick will require you to handle your cat more than most of the other tricks in the book, so before beginning, make sure you have desensitized your cat to being handled. If your cat is one that simply will not tolerate being handled, then you may want to move on to another trick that involves less touching and physical manipulation.

Level of difficulty:

🐾 🐾 🐾

What you will need:
a clicker and treats

Length of session:
three to five minutes

Frequency of sessions:
once every day

Advance preparation:
none

Previous tricks required:
Down, Snuggle, and comfort with being handled

1. Ask your cat to go into a "Down" position on a large tabletop or on the floor. Make sure that the cat has ample room, and that there is no danger of its falling. Consider placing a tablecloth or blanket down on the surface that you are working the cat on, to make it more comfortable. If you have any

trouble convincing the cat to go into the "Down" position,
go back and review that trick before continuing.

2. Position your-
self in front of
the cat. Show
it the treat you
are holding (it
might help to
use an absolute-
ly irresistible
treat, such as
baby food with
tuna mixed in);

move it right to the cat's nose if necessary to pique its interest, but do not let it break the "Down" position. Then, slowly
move the treat to the left of the cat's head, while gently
pushing the cat over onto its side with your right hand.
While doing so, make sure to say "Play Dead." At first the
cat may object to being pushed over onto its side; distracting

it with the treat
while you push it
over will help take
its mind off of
your manipula-
tions. As soon as
you have success-
fully moved the
cat over onto its
side, click the

clicker and let the cat have the treat (you should learn to hold the clicker in your dominant hand, between the thumb and the base of your index finger; this will allow you to still use that hand to manipulate the cat). Work this step until the cat comfort-ably goes over onto its side for you, and begins to real-ize that doing so brings on the reward.

3. Gradually, as the cat begins to understand what you want, use less and less hand pressure to push the cat over onto its side. Eventually, just a light touch on its back should be enough to prompt the desired action. Continue to lighten up the touch until you are not making contact at all, but instead merely moving your hand above and over the cat's back. This motion becomes the hand signal for the trick. Be patient; this will take a good number of short ses-sions to accomplish. Continue to use the treat as a tempta-tion, and always click and reward when successful.

4. After your cat achieves the "Play Dead" on the table or floor, try working it in different rooms and on dif-ferent surfaces—perhaps the bed, sofa, or coffee table.

Trick No. 26
Roll Over

Sometimes cats will spontaneously begin performing tricks they know just to get attention or a reward, and my cat Riley is no exception. I once used him in a shoot for a *Wee Sing* children's music video series. All Riley had to do was sit in a chair while a group of children close by danced and sang some songs. Riley ended up getting a little bored with it all, and began trying to get my attention. He started rolling over and over in the chair, all on his own, hoping that a treat would be forthcoming. I didn't give him a treat for that, but I thought it was awfully cute, and a good example of how smart cats really are.

Take your time with this trick. Nervous, skittish cats probably won't feel comfortable

Level of difficulty:
🐾 🐾 🐾

What you will need:
a clicker and treats

Length of session:
three to five minutes

Frequency of sessions:
once every day

Advance preparation:
none

Previous tricks required:
Down, Play Dead

rolling over, so only attempt it if you have a confident, well-socialized cat that likes to be handled. You must first make sure the cat is able to do a perfect "Down" before attempting the "Roll Over."

1. Ask your cat to go into a "Down" position on a large table top or on the floor. There should be enough room for the cat to roll over without the possibility of falling off the table. Placing a tablecloth or rug down first might make it more comfortable for the cat. Make sure it is comfortable, secure, and hungry.

2. Position yourself on your cat's left (with the cat facing you), and reach over the cat with your left hand to show the cat the treat. Get it interested without having it break the "Down" position. Then slowly rotate the treat up and over the cat's head so that it follows the treat around with his or her head. At this point also give the command "Roll Over."

3. As you move the treat in an arc over the cat's head with your left hand, use your right hand to gently guide the cat over onto its side. Then continue to rotate the treat around so that the cat goes onto its back and then onto its other side. Momentum is the key; try to get the cat to do this in one fluid motion. When you do succeed, click

your clicker and reward your cat. Success will take some time to achieve. With many cats, you may have to first perfect just having the cat go on its side. That's fine; there is no need to rush. Always click and reward any positive results.

4. After working this for a while, you will develop a feel for just how much physical manipulation is needed. Some cats will get it quickly after you guide them through the roll once or twice with your hand. Others will take longer. The main difficulty with this trick is that cats are not too fond of being on their backs for very long.

5. Eventually you should use less and less hand manipulation. The cat will begin to understand what is being asked of it. Attempt to increase your distance from the cat once it is rolling over well. Ultimately the treat, the verbal command, and your circular hand motion should be enough to elicit a roll over from the cat.

6. Work this trick for one or two sessions each day. It may take several weeks to master it, though cats that like being handled may learn it quickly.

Remember: Never force a cat to do anything!

TRICK No. 27
CRAWL

Teaching this trick will take some patience on your part. The objective will be for you to get the cat to do a "commando crawl" type movement across the floor for a short distance, as if it were going under a low obstruction.

1. Begin with your cat in a "Down" position. If possible, it is best to work this trick on a rug on the floor.

Level of difficulty:

🐾 🐾 🐾

What you will need:
a clicker and treats

Length of session:
three to four minutes

Frequency of sessions:
once or twice every day

Advance preparation:
none

Previous trick required:
Down

2. Hold a treat about one or two inches in front of your cat. Crouch down, rather than stand; you want to encourage forward motion, not vertical. Lure the cat toward you slowly, with the food. You will have to experiment with treat speed; too fast and the cat will rise up and walk, too slow and the cat may reach out for the treat or pounce. As you begin luring the cat, say the cat's name and then "Crawl." Be patient;

it may be a while before the cat figures out what you are asking. The pulling-away move-ment of the treat becomes the hand signal for "Crawl."

3. When the cat does begin to crawl, let it go four or five inches, then click once and reward. Work this stage for several days until you can reliably get the cat to crawl a short distance.

4. To get the cat to crawl longer distances, delay the click and reward for a bit longer each time, until the cat is traveling several feet before receiv-ing them.

5. The last step is to get the cat to crawl while you are located several feet away from it when the trick begins. Very gradually increase your distance from the cat when asking it to "Crawl." Use the hand signal and verbal command. If you succeed, give both of you a treat and a pat on the back.

The "Crawl" is one of those tricks that will involve a lot of treat manipulation on your part, and lots of trial and error. By now, though, you have probably learned to modify techniques and timing slightly to fit your cat's personality and its desire to work. That's the real key to training any animal—knowing its capabilities, and knowing what it really responds to.

Remember to click and reward as soon as the cat performs the desired action!

Trick No. 28
Jump to Shoulder

In order to properly work this trick, your cat will need a high food drive. It must also like being physically close to people. You will need the services of your trusty helper, who may want to wear a jacket or heavy shirt for this one. The objective is to lure the cat into jumping onto someone's shoulder from wherever it is, on command.

Level of difficulty:

What you will need:
a clicker, treats, a helper, and a heavy shirt

Length of session:
two to five minutes

Frequency of sessions:
once every day

Advance preparation:
none

Previous trick required:
Jump into Lap

1. Start the trick with the cat up high on a filing cabinet or bookshelf—anywhere that is close to the level of your helper's shoulders. Have the helper stand about one foot away from the cat, facing away from it. You should be in front of your helper, holding a treat directly over his or her shoulder.

2. Say "Jump" as you attempt to tantalize the cat with the treat; the objective is to coax the cat onto your helper's shoulder. Make sure the helper is close enough at this point so that the cat can easily step

over instead of having to jump. If necessary, move the treat closer to the cat's nose, then bait it toward the helper's shoulder. Even if the cat puts just one foot on the helper's

shoulder, click and reward. Continue to work this step until you can reliably get the cat to walk over onto your helper's shoulder.

3. Gradually increase the distance between your helper and the cat. There will be a point at which the cat will no longer be able to step over; it will need to jump onto the shoulder in order to get the treat.

This will be the crucial moment; when the cat does jump, click, reward, and really praise. Continue working this step until the cat will reliably and comfortably jump a two- or three-foot distance from the shelf or cabinet to the helper's shoulder.

4. The next step is to slowly decrease the height of the cat's launching point. Go from the filing cabinet to a table top, or if using a bookshelf, simply go down to the next lower one. Make sure to use a very gradual descent as the cat will become confused and lose interest if the drop is too sudden.

Also, when you do begin to decrease the height of the launching point, have your helper come back in a bit closer at first. Then gradually increase the distance again. Eventually you want the cat to be able to jump up onto the helper's shoulder from the floor. Always give the command "Jump," and always click and reward a successful attempt.

5. Continue working the "Jump," only now have the helper face the cat (don't attempt this until the cat is great at doing this trick from behind the helper, so that it doesn't veer to one side and scratch the helper's face). Eventually the cat should be able to jump up onto the shoulder whether the helper is turned away from or toward the cat.

6. After perfecting the "Jump" onto the shoulder, begin working it in reverse. Teach the cat to jump from the shoulder to the filing cabinet, to the table, to a chair, and then to the floor. Or teach it to jump from one person's shoulder to another's.

TRICK No. 29
OPEN CUPBOARD

Cats are extremely curious by nature, and often stick their whiskers into the darnedest places in their never-ending quest to explore. Your cat may have already learned to open a cupboard or door (often to your dismay) to get to something desirable on the other side, perhaps a bag of food or a choice empty can of tuna. This behavior can be shaped into a trick that is performed on command. Be forewarned however that, once your cat does learn this trick, it may be hard to stop!

To teach this trick to your cat, you will need a cupboard with a protruding handle,

Level of difficulty:

What you will need:
a clicker, strip treats (a piece of cooked liver or jerky), and a kitchen cupboard

Length of session:
three to five minutes

Frequency of sessions:
once every day

Advance preparation:
secure treat strip inside cupboard

Previous tricks required:
Shake, Wave, and perhaps Ring It

preferably one that is near the floor. You will also need to use
a type of treat that has a bit more durability to it than tuna,
cheese, or baby food. A strip of cooked liver or jerky, preferably one that is at least four to five inches long, should work
well. You will also need to use your clicker for this trick.

1. Before involving the cat at all, you will need to set
up the trick properly. Open the kitchen cupboard
and devise some way of securing the treat strip so that, with
the cupboard open slightly (about an inch), it will protrude
about half an inch beyond the door. Try using a clothespin
to secure the treat strip to some item inside, perhaps a cere-
al box or large book. It should be secured well enough so
that your cat cannot pull it out with its teeth. This treat will
act to tease your cat into pawing at the slightly open cupboard; with luck and some patience, your cat will eventually
(and accidentally) open it further, whereupon you will click
and reward.

2. Once you have the treat strip secured properly (stick-
ing out about a half-inch from the open door),
bring your cat into the
kitchen and
show it the pro-
truding end of
the treat. Be
patient; you want
the cat to begin
pawing at the
treat. Encourage
the cat by tapping
on the treat while

repeatedly saying "Open." As soon as the cat begins to paw
(even if it doesn't touch the treat or door), click and reward.
Work on this step until you can consistently get your cat to
paw at the protruding treat when you give the command
"Open." Work this step once or twice each day, when the cat
is very hungry.

3. Begin to
slowly
move the treat
strip farther into
the slightly open
cupboard, while
you continue to
work Step Two.
Eventually, you
want to move the
treat strip all the

way inside the cupboard. It should still be visible to the cat,
though, through the open door. Don't forget to click and
reward each time the cat paws at the treat or cupboard door.

4. Continue working the trick, but begin closing the
cupboard door. At this point, you will want to begin
encouraging the cat to actually move the door open. Any
time the cat does move the door (even slightly), click and
reward. Begin attempting to position the cat so that it is to
the side of the door rather than facing it head-on. Ideally, for
the cat to open the door, it will need to use the paw opposite
that door. If you want the cat to open the left-side cupboard
door, for example, encourage the cat to be just to the right

of it, pawing at it with its *right* foot. If the cat uses its left foot, it might end up *closing* the door instead of opening it. This will be the hardest part of teaching the trick.

You may find that the cat will accidentally do exactly what you are asking of it; when this happens, click and reward! Remember not to overwork the cat; instead, shape the behavior over several weeks, using short, positive sessions each time.

5. Eventually, you should close the cupboard door completely, with the treat still inside. In order for the cat to open the door at this point, it will have to direct its pawing at the door handle. Whenever this happens (even if the door doesn't open), click and reward. Keep at it; there will be a magic moment when your cat actually opens the door with

its paw. When this happens, click, reward, and then love the cat up. Continue working the trick once each day until you can reliably get the cat to open the cupboard door just by your tapping on it and saying "Open." Make sure, of course, that there is a treat waiting for it inside. If you succeed in teaching this "Open" command to your cat, then you truly have become a cat trainer!

Trick No. 30
Fetch

Yes, you can teach your cat to fetch, but don't expect it to be in hot competition with the golden retriever down the street. This trick may take weeks or months to teach, and might be the hardest in the book. If you decide to tackle it, be patient!

Level of difficulty:

What you will need:
a clicker, regular and gooey treats, a sound-making device, and a toy or ball

Length of session:
three to four minutes

Frequency of sessions:
once or twice every day

Advance preparation:
none

Previous tricks required:
Play Ball, Come

Some cats will be more motivated than others to perform this trick. Success with the "Fetch" command in cats is to a certain degree dependent on the level of prey drive in the animal. If your cat has a toy that it is particularly crazy about and likes to chase after, then you may have excellent results. If your cat doesn't have this toy motivation, it may not respond well.

1. Find a toy that your cat will love to play with and stalk. A ball made of cloth or yarn should do nicely. Make sure it isn't more than two or three inches in diameter so that the cat can easily hold it in its mouth. This differs from the play ball trick, in which the ball used should be too large for the cat to fit in its mouth. Don't use anything with catnip in it, as this will break the cat's focus and make it act like a goof ball. The texture of the toy is important, as well; it should be relatively soft and easy to grasp. Avoid using a hard toy or a rubber ball, unless your cat has already developed a lust for a toy like this. Some cats won't hold a hard plastic toy in their mouths.

2. Place the cat in front of you or next to you. Tease it with the toy for a few seconds, until it becomes excited. Then toss the toy about two to four feet away; say the cat's name and then "Fetch." Most cats will go for the toy and perhaps grab it with their paws. If your cat does this, immediately click once and reward. If

necessary, toss the treat to the cat, while it remains halfway across the room with the toy. Don't worry about the cat bringing the toy back to you just yet.

3. The next step ensures that the cat regularly puts the toy into its mouth. You can do this by smearing some food on the toy. Some

cats will be too distracted by the food on the toy to think at all, however; if yours is one of these cats, then forego the use of food here, and allow the toy itself to be the reward. Work on this step until

the cat is reliably going to the toy and putting it in its mouth. Remember not to throw the toy more than a few feet away right now.

4. Once the cat is consistently putting the toy in its mouth, try calling the cat to you. If the cat even *looks* at you when you call it, click and reward. Keep working this until you get the cat to come to you. If you are having trouble getting the cat to return to you, try using your whistle or buzzer; if you have already taught the "Come" trick, then the cat may readily come back to you. If so, click and reward generously. Don't click and reward if the cat returns half-way, then wanders off. Have patience; this step may take some time. *Never* use a leash to reel the cat in to you, as some cat books recommend. The cat will resist and panic, and may never trust you again. Remember, in order to learn, a cat has to *want* to do something.

5. Once you have the cat returning to you with the toy in its mouth, try gradually increasing the distance between yourself and the cat. Eventually you should be able to get the cat to go out across the room, pick up the toy, and return to you. Then try using a similar toy, perhaps something with the same shape, but of a different color or texture. Over time, change the items until the cat is retrieving a wide spectrum of things, from balls to socks to crumpled paper. Be sure to reward your cat for mastering such a difficult trick.

Linking Tricks Together

Once your cat has learned a number of the tricks in this book, it will be possible to link some of them together to create an impressive display of feline intelligence.

When you start linking tricks together, you should get your cat first to perform one and then the other; and then to try doing so with a seamless continuity between the two. For instance, if you want to link the "Jump into Lap" trick with "Kiss," you would first perfect each separately; then you'd have the cat perform one followed by the other; and then you'd begin reducing the time between the two until these really became one trick in the cat's mind. This technique is called "patterning." Cats learn patterns very easily, provided you do not confuse them by changing the order of desired behaviors. Though the cat will eventually learn to perform two tricks together in seamless unity, you should still use the appropriate command at the appropriate time. When the cat arrives at a point in the linked trick when it must sit, give the "Sit" command; when it comes to the part requiring it to go through a tunnel, say "Through."

You have in fact already been linking the "Stay" command to the "Sit" and "Down" commands. Try the "Stay" with the "Stand" command as well. Give any of these commands and then follow it with the "Stay" command.

Be inventive. The "Come" and the "Come Mark" can easily be combined, as can the "Rub It" and "Speak," the "Through" and "Over," and the "Come Mark" and "Wash It." Just be patient, and realize that when you combine tricks, it will be as if you are teaching one entirely new trick to your cat. You will be testing the limits of your cat's concentration as well, so take your time.

A FINAL WORD

I wrote this book to show how smart cats really are and to provide you with new ways to deepen your relationship with your cat, while providing many hours of fun and enjoyment for both of you. I hope I have accomplished these objectives. Remember that you are training your cat for fun and not out of necessity; enjoy yourselves, and keep a lighthearted attitude throughout.

Don't let this book be the limiting factor in your cat's "education." At this stage, you yourself have become a cat trainer; there is no reason you cannot invent tricks of your own to teach your cat. Just think each one out carefully, make sure it suits your cat's personality, and don't let it be in any way dangerous to your cat. Most important, make sure you both have fun!

Index

ABOUT THE AUTHORS

Anne Gordon is a native of the Puget Sound area in western Washington. Originally a zookeeper at Seattle's Woodland Park Zoo, she was the first female to work directly with large carnivores. Anne now owns and operates Annie's Animal Actors, an agency that provides and prepares animals of every type for film, television, commercial productions, and print advertising. Anne was the principal supplier of trained animals for *Northern Exposure*, has worked on the set of *Rescue 911*, and has provided trained cats for many feature films, including Disney's *Homeward Bound*, *The Good Son*, *Home for the Holidays*, and *Georgia*. She also has been seen on many television shows.

Anne has taught canine obedience and tricks classes, and she spent five years lecturing on endangered species and native northwestern animals. She shares her home with five cats, nine dogs, a mule deer, and two rescued wolves.

Writer and animal behaviorist **Steve Duno** is the author of *Choosing a Dog: Your Guide to Picking the Perfect Breed for Your Lifestyle* and *Leader of the Pack*. A native New Yorker, he currently resides in Seattle, Washington.